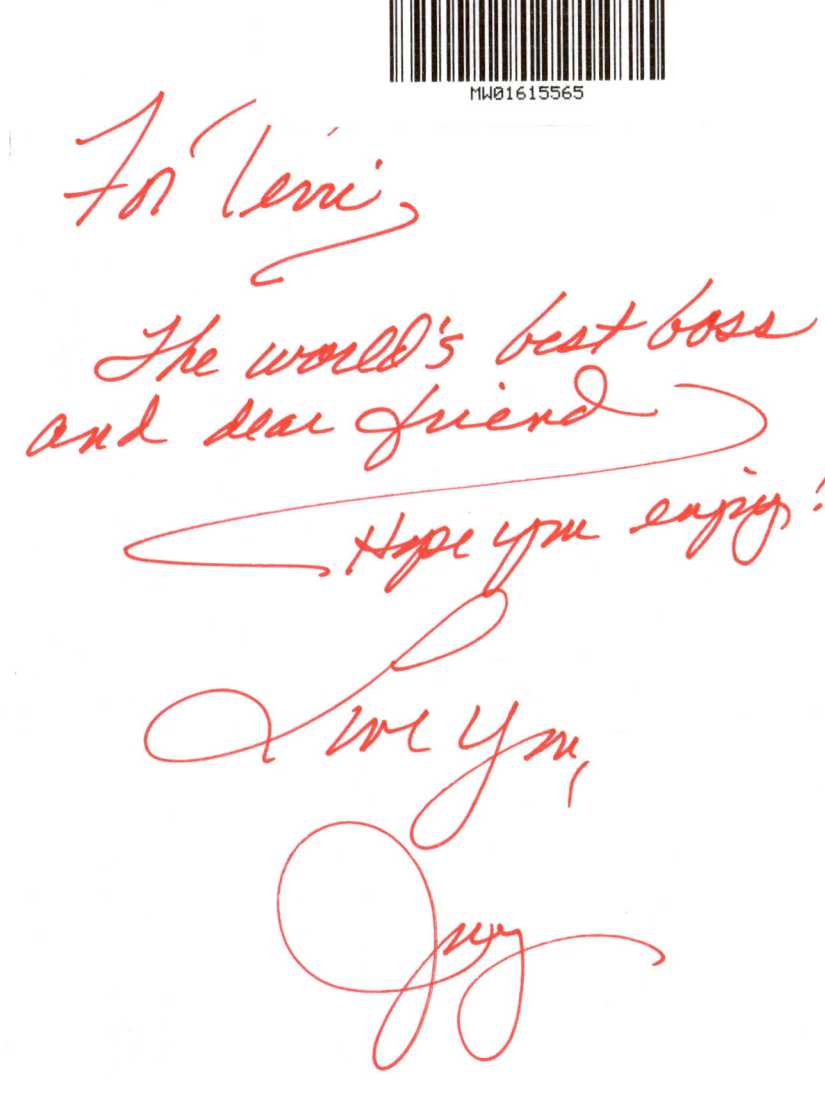

For Terri,

The world's best boss
and dear friend

Hope you enjoy!

Love You,

Jay

GRASSHOPPER CIRCLING

BY

JOY JONES

Copyright © 2012 by Joy Jones
Edited by Judy Robinson
Cover Design by Sandi Wright
Photography by Robin Levin and Ron Marchese

ISBN 978-0-7414-7559-6 Paperback
ISBN 978-0-7414-7560-2 eBook
Library of Congress Control Number: 2012937428

Printed in the United States of America

Published June 2012

INFINITY PUBLISHING
1094 New DeHaven Street, Suite 100
West Conshohocken, PA 19428-2713
Toll-free (877) BUY BOOK
Local Phone (610) 941-9999
Fax (610) 941-9959
Info@buybooksontheweb.com
www.buybooksontheweb.com

PREFACE

This sequel to *Higher Ground, One Woman's Journey,* is the book that for years I had no appetite to write. Nevertheless, eventually I did. How typical of me! Circles. I do circles......like a grasshopper within that circle, leaping from one place and person and plan to another......thus its title, *Grasshopper, Circling.*

From 1995 to 2001 were the 'Brian years'. We lived and loved in first Arizona, then Texas. Ours was an imperfect relationship, but it had many perks for us both. Brian's daughters, Cathy and Chris, will remain forever in my heart. Getting to know Brian's lifelong friend Henry and his wife Donna was a plus. Our travels took me to the eastern part of the United States for the first time. And, Brian's mother, Hilda, was an all-time favorite character. Yes, our marriage didn't make it. Nevertheless, the memories of our years together bring me much happiness. Brian died of cancer in 2010.

As in *Higher Ground,* I tell my stories with transpersonal psychology woven throughout them. My hope is that readers will gain some insight into how they show up for their own lives. If so, my effort to be completely honest is rewarded.

CHAPTER ONE

Fall, 1995

'The Golden Girls We Weren't'

I wasn't lying. I just wasn't telling the whole truth. I was certified in all social studies subjects in Texas, so teaching government to seniors was covered legally. What I didn't mention, and the principal of Eisenhower High School didn't know, was that I had never in my twenty plus years' experience taught a government course. However, as I sat there in the principal's office, smiling confidently and being my professional best, I first felt the lack of confidence in myself that would stay with me all fall semester, and it would rob me of my usual enjoyment of teaching.

Nothing so far, since my move back last week to Houston from Sedona, AZ was evidence of the affirmation I had recited over and over during the long road trip on Interstate 10: "God's way for me is joyous, a way of safety and security. I give thanks that I now walk in paths of pleasantness, prosperity and peace. The boundless, limitless power that created the universe is now accomplishing in and through me all that is for my highest good in mind, body and affairs. I give thanks that I am divinely equipped to accomplish great things with ease."

My memories of Cameron and her home in northwest Houston were immediately challenged. Yes, her two story, brick home, with the pool in the backyard, was even more beautiful than I remembered, but the property, inside and out, was wrapped in an energy that felt chilling and somehow unsafe. Cameron had made ready four of the five upstairs rooms: a bedroom, bath, TV sitting room, and an office. Every inch of wall, and desk, dresser, and bathroom counter surface was cluttered with decorative items. This, at least, was what I recalled. I had once told Cameron that she could never move because it would take an 18 wheeler to hold all her furniture, dried flower arrangements, lamps, pictures, books, paintings, pillows, dishes, and art objects. Therefore, I felt cramped, even though I certainly was not. The walls had a way of closing in on me. I have always preferred space, just for the sake of space. Now, I realized, I needed some measure of emptiness for my peace of mind.

And, Cameron wasn't the same either. For five years, before I had left Houston for Arizona in 1990, we had been close friends. As head of the Study Skills Dept. at Cypress Creek High School, she was my immediate boss. Our relationship had gone easily from professional to personal. We were like sisters. We took a Christmas vacation together; she was often a guest in my home, and we had shared our secrets, regrets, hopes, and dreams with each other. I knew from the moment I went to work for her that her marriage to the Romanian ex-Olympic soccer star and current Cy Creek soccer coach was an ongoing saga of trauma drama, thus I had not been surprised that she was just recently divorced from him. Actually, I thought it was a healthy development for her life. Now, I was sure, she would lose the extra weight she had put on and would return to her model self. She was tiny in statue, and she had the most welcoming face: large, friendly, blue eyes; a smile that was genuine; blond hair that could be styled from sophisticated to casual by her expert hand, and a complexion that went from peaches and cream to bronze glow in the summertime.

Then, two days after moving in, I slipped and fell down the stairs in Cameron's house. I couldn't stay in bed. I couldn't. I had hit Houston in a dead run to get a teaching job. The traditional week of teacher inservice had begun, so I had to ignore my pain and the horrible Houston heat and get hired somewhere. Nothing felt good and I wasn't living the happy days I had anticipated last week as I drove toward Texas. I was taking a teaching assignment I knew very little about, and Eisenhower High School was a difficult drive from Cameron's house because Houston traffic had worsened in the past six years. However, these two realities didn't stop me from saying yes, and thankfully, to the job offer. As long as it wasn't algebra or chemistry, I figured I could teach it. Nevertheless, even before I entered the classroom on the first day of school, I felt the fear of being unprepared to teach government to 95% black senior students.

Too, it wasn't happening like I thought it would at Cameron's. 'The Golden Girls', we weren't. Sure we had the 'girl talks', but I never felt like anything I said really had any long lasting, positive effect on Cameron. And too, even after all those years in Sedona where my main focus was on growing spiritually, I still found myself fighting my tendency to be judgmental of her behavior. Consequently, I didn't feel like we were any genuine help to each other, like on the popular TV show.

"I don't care what you say, Bonn, I am telling you right now that I am never going to get involved with a man again." Cameron was cleaning the pool and my plan to relax on the patio lounge and look at the sky and think my thoughts was shot to hell.

"You don't think you are involved with a man right now?" I countered with what I hoped was camouflaged irritation.

"Damn it, Bonn. You know what I mean. Sometimes you make me so mad. Just because all the men in your life have treated you like a queen and never abused you, you think that any woman who puts up with torment is just plain stupid. And I really hate it when you claim that the people we attract into our lives have to do most with what it is we need to learn about ourselves. That is bullshit, as far as I'm concerned."

So I dive right in, just like a hundred times before. Like I really think that saying it one more time will cause Cameron to change her way of thinking, thus behaving. One would think that I think that I have all the right answers.

"Cameron, we are intuitively drawn to the person who has what we don't have, what we lost, what got hurt, or was never developed in childhood. So we establish a relationship with someone and stay connected to that person because we want to develop that missing component in ourselves. This isn't just my idea. Re-read Kingma's book, *The Future of Love,* for proof. But, for the sake of discussion, let's take me for example. I don't have the willingness to allow for difference, and although all the books demand it, I can't seem to come from a position of unconditional love with my mates. If they can't dance; read the books I do; enjoy everything from opera to playing dominos in Shiner, TX; engage in long hours of analyzing behavior, or are willing to start a whole new life someplace else - on a dime, then they have failed the test and I must move on. Consequently, I have attracted man after man who doesn't meet all my requirements (like there is one who could). Yet, none of them have demanded that I be like them. In fact, my differences are attractive to them. So bottom line, they have had the unconditional love for me that I haven't had for them. Therefore, I will keep attracting these men until I change who I am. It isn't about them, it is about me."

Cameron was silent and staying busy cleaning the pool. I was beginning to think that this familiar round was being cut short when she said, "Okay, I can see why you can apply this theory to your life, but I don't see how it relates to mine. Can you tell me why all the men in my life, beginning with my dad, have treated me like shit? They all have, every damn one of them, been unappreciative of my love and they didn't value who I was. There was always some criticism: I needed to lose weight; I needed to be on time; I needed to change the way I dressed or wore my hair; I needed to give them more space, I needed to, I needed to, I needed to." Her voice got louder and angrier with each word.

I was not enjoying this conversation, but I plunged on. "It seems to me, Babe, that from what I know about your life, you have spent it trying to please in order to feel loved. Beginning with your dad, you have swallowed a shit-load of abuse all your life. You taught all these men how to treat you by excusing their degrading behavior because you needed their love. Therefore, these men are a mirror for you. They reflect the way you think about yourself. If you had healthy love and respect for yourself, you wouldn't allow them to mistreat you in the hopes of getting the love you want. My favorite definition for insanity is, 'To keep doing what you are doing, yet expect a different result.' If you are ever going to get past this way of being in relationships, you have to be in one. That's why I say that you and I have to be in romantic relationships if we are to ever change the way we have always been. It's like getting back into the saddle once we realize there is a better way to ride."

Cameron tossed aside the pool net with a vengeance. As she walked to the back door she slung over her shoulder a parting shot, "You do know that the least attractive thing about you is how you can make any subject, regardless of how heartfelt, be antiseptic. You wipe everything clean of any feelings. You admit to not having unconditional love? Maybe you should make that a bit broader to include LOVE......period." One more round, until another day.

But thank God for the backyard pool. It was saving my sanity. Every late afternoon, I would swim until I was tired. Then I would crawl up onto the float and stare at the city sky and remember. I'd remember Klint, the man I didn't marry five years earlier, and more recently Brian, the married man who had rescued me from the winter snow outside of

Flagstaff only five months ago. My plan to forget both these men wasn't happening. Both of them had followed me to Texas. And Klint. Klint showed no sign of ever going away. The memory of our last time together in Flagstaff, back in 1994, played over and over in my head. The water kept me cool, but not my thoughts.

* * * * *

"How in the world are you?" Klint never failed to begin a phone conversation with this question. His throaty, slow, southern voice and his words were instantly familiar.

"My lord, Klint! What a surprise. Where are you?" I was opening the refrigerator door to get out the week's leftovers for yet another meal, but changed my mind and closed it.

"I'm here in Flagstaff on my way back to Oklahoma from Ventura. What ya doin for dinner?"

"You're in town? How in the world did you find me?"

A brief silence and then he said, "You know I always know where you are."

"Oh right. Come on, how did you know?"

"I'll tell you over dinner. How 'bout it?"

"Dinner and what else, you rascal?"

"That's up to you sweetie, but you know what I'd like."

"I do." I was smiling at the memory of our nights those six months we lived together in Houston before I broke it off. "And, you know what I'd like. I'll pack my toothbrush and meet you where in about an hour?"

As I danced my way into the bathroom, I could almost taste the wonderful time we had had last year when I was invited to be his guest at the Potentate Ball in Muskogee, OK. I just love it, was my thought, as I stepped into the shower. Klint's effect on me hadn't changed with time. It had been five years since I had called off our wedding, yet

GRASSHOPPER CIRCLING

BY

JOY JONES

INFINITY
PUBLISHING

Copyright © 2012 by Joy Jones
Edited by Judy Robinson
Cover Design by Sandi Wright
Photography by Robin Levin and Ron Marchese

ISBN 978-0-7414-7559-6 Paperback
ISBN 978-0-7414-7560-2 eBook
Library of Congress Control Number: 2012937428

Printed in the United States of America

Published June 2012

INFINITY PUBLISHING
1094 New DeHaven Street, Suite 100
West Conshohocken, PA 19428-2713
Toll-free (877) BUY BOOK
Local Phone (610) 941-9999
Fax (610) 941-9959
Info@buybooksontheweb.com
www.buybooksontheweb.com

This book is dedicated to the memory of

BRIAN BERWALD

March 23, 1938 – February 26, 2010

PREFACE

This sequel to *Higher Ground, One Woman's Journey,* is the book that for years I had no appetite to write. Nevertheless, eventually I did. How typical of me! Circles. I do circles......like a grasshopper within that circle, leaping from one place and person and plan to another......thus its title, *Grasshopper, Circling.*

From 1995 to 2001 were the 'Brian years'. We lived and loved in first Arizona, then Texas. Ours was an imperfect relationship, but it had many perks for us both. Brian's daughters, Cathy and Chris, will remain forever in my heart. Getting to know Brian's lifelong friend Henry and his wife Donna was a plus. Our travels took me to the eastern part of the United States for the first time. And, Brian's mother, Hilda, was an all-time favorite character. Yes, our marriage didn't make it. Nevertheless, the memories of our years together bring me much happiness. Brian died of cancer in 2010.

As in *Higher Ground,* I tell my stories with transpersonal psychology woven throughout them. My hope is that readers will gain some insight into how they show up for their own lives. If so, my effort to be completely honest is rewarded.

CHAPTER ONE

Fall, 1995

'The Golden Girls We Weren't'

I wasn't lying. I just wasn't telling the whole truth. I was certified in all social studies subjects in Texas, so teaching government to seniors was covered legally. What I didn't mention, and the principal of Eisenhower High School didn't know, was that I had never in my twenty plus years' experience taught a government course. However, as I sat there in the principal's office, smiling confidently and being my professional best, I first felt the lack of confidence in myself that would stay with me all fall semester, and it would rob me of my usual enjoyment of teaching.

Nothing so far, since my move back last week to Houston from Sedona, AZ was evidence of the affirmation I had recited over and over during the long road trip on Interstate 10: "God's way for me is joyous, a way of safety and security. I give thanks that I now walk in paths of pleasantness, prosperity and peace. The boundless, limitless power that created the universe is now accomplishing in and through me all that is for my highest good in mind, body and affairs. I give thanks that I am divinely equipped to accomplish great things with ease."

My memories of Cameron and her home in northwest Houston were immediately challenged. Yes, her two story, brick home, with the pool in the backyard, was even more beautiful than I remembered, but the property, inside and out, was wrapped in an energy that felt chilling and somehow unsafe. Cameron had made ready four of the five upstairs rooms: a bedroom, bath, TV sitting room, and an office. Every inch of wall, and desk, dresser, and bathroom counter surface was cluttered with decorative items. This, at least, was what I recalled. I had once told Cameron that she could never move because it would take an 18 wheeler to hold all her furniture, dried flower arrangements, lamps, pictures, books, paintings, pillows, dishes, and art objects. Therefore, I felt cramped, even though I certainly was not. The walls had a way of closing in on me. I have always preferred space, just for the sake of space. Now, I realized, I needed some measure of emptiness for my peace of mind.

And, Cameron wasn't the same either. For five years, before I had left Houston for Arizona in 1990, we had been close friends. As head of the Study Skills Dept. at Cypress Creek High School, she was my immediate boss. Our relationship had gone easily from professional to personal. We were like sisters. We took a Christmas vacation together; she was often a guest in my home, and we had shared our secrets, regrets, hopes, and dreams with each other. I knew from the moment I went to work for her that her marriage to the Romanian ex-Olympic soccer star and current Cy Creek soccer coach was an ongoing saga of trauma drama, thus I had not been surprised that she was just recently divorced from him. Actually, I thought it was a healthy development for her life. Now, I was sure, she would lose the extra weight she had put on and would return to her model self. She was tiny in statue, and she had the most welcoming face: large, friendly, blue eyes; a smile that was genuine; blond hair that could be styled from sophisticated to casual by her expert hand, and a complexion that went from peaches and cream to bronze glow in the summertime.

Then, two days after moving in, I slipped and fell down the stairs in Cameron's house. I couldn't stay in bed. I couldn't. I had hit Houston in a dead run to get a teaching

4

job. The traditional week of teacher inservice had begun, so I had to ignore my pain and the horrible Houston heat and get hired somewhere. Nothing felt good and I wasn't living the happy days I had anticipated last week as I drove toward Texas. I was taking a teaching assignment I knew very little about, and Eisenhower High School was a difficult drive from Cameron's house because Houston traffic had worsened in the past six years. However, these two realities didn't stop me from saying yes, and thankfully, to the job offer. As long as it wasn't algebra or chemistry, I figured I could teach it. Nevertheless, even before I entered the classroom on the first day of school, I felt the fear of being unprepared to teach government to 95% black senior students.

Too, it wasn't happening like I thought it would at Cameron's. 'The Golden Girls', we weren't. Sure we had the 'girl talks', but I never felt like anything I said really had any long lasting, positive effect on Cameron. And too, even after all those years in Sedona where my main focus was on growing spiritually, I still found myself fighting my tendency to be judgmental of her behavior. Consequently, I didn't feel like we were any genuine help to each other, like on the popular TV show.

"I don't care what you say, Bonn, I am telling you right now that I am never going to get involved with a man again." Cameron was cleaning the pool and my plan to relax on the patio lounge and look at the sky and think my thoughts was shot to hell.

"You don't think you are involved with a man right now?" I countered with what I hoped was camouflaged irritation.

"Damn it, Bonn. You know what I mean. Sometimes you make me so mad. Just because all the men in your life have treated you like a queen and never abused you, you think that any woman who puts up with torment is just plain stupid. And I really hate it when you claim that the people we attract into our lives have to do most with what it is we need to learn about ourselves. That is bullshit, as far as I'm concerned."

So I dive right in, just like a hundred times before. Like I really think that saying it one more time will cause Cameron to change her way of thinking, thus behaving. One would think that I think that I have all the right answers.

"Cameron, we are intuitively drawn to the person who has what we don't have, what we lost, what got hurt, or was never developed in childhood. So we establish a relationship with someone and stay connected to that person because we want to develop that missing component in ourselves. This isn't just my idea. Re-read Kingma's book, *The Future of Love,* for proof. But, for the sake of discussion, let's take me for example. I don't have the willingness to allow for difference, and although all the books demand it, I can't seem to come from a position of unconditional love with my mates. If they can't dance; read the books I do; enjoy everything from opera to playing dominos in Shiner, TX; engage in long hours of analyzing behavior, or are willing to start a whole new life someplace else - on a dime, then they have failed the test and I must move on. Consequently, I have attracted man after man who doesn't meet all my requirements (like there is one who could). Yet, none of them have demanded that I be like them. In fact, my differences are attractive to them. So bottom line, they have had the unconditional love for me that I haven't had for them. Therefore, I will keep attracting these men until I change who I am. It isn't about them, it is about me."

Cameron was silent and staying busy cleaning the pool. I was beginning to think that this familiar round was being cut short when she said, "Okay, I can see why you can apply this theory to your life, but I don't see how it relates to mine. Can you tell me why all the men in my life, beginning with my dad, have treated me like shit? They all have, every damn one of them, been unappreciative of my love and they didn't the memory of the last time we were together had my heart thumping wildly.

I had flown into Tulsa, and he was waiting for me. As always he was dressed the same: Stetson hat, western shirt and jeans on his still-slim body; gold chains from the Middle East around his neck and wrist; large rings that called attention to his years with Shell Oil and being a 32 degree Mason; expensive cowboy boots, and that crooked smile that warned me I could be in trouble again.

His kiss reminded me of our first one that morning in Santa Rosa, NM in the late 1980's. Tentative, yet sure. And, he didn't rush to words. I knew he was reading my mind. He always had.

I spoke first. "Well, you haven't aged one bit, dadgum your hide." I laughed and coughed at the same time.

"And, I'm sure you know you haven't either," was his quick response. "Most likely, we are saving ourselves for each other," he chuckled.

"You would start right in on me, wouldn't you? What's the matter? Running short of folks to terrorize?" What was wrong with my voice? I couldn't talk without clearing my throat. A sure sign that I was nervous.

"Sweetheart." He took my bag, and started me towards the exit. "You have no idea how many people are waiting to meet you." His habit of changing the subject was still in tact, and I could never tell if it was because he hadn't heard what I said; didn't understand what I had said, or was just ignoring me. At that moment, it didn't matter at all. I was so glad to see him, and I knew he knew I was.

Many years later he would tell me how, for months, he was teased by his Shriner friends about how often we changed our clothes that weekend. I didn't realize it, but after every time spent alone in our hotel room, we must have reappeared wearing something different. The chemistry between us made us willing slaves to our hormones, and the celebration atmosphere of the occasion created a magical two days.

The Shriner Potentate, Greg Schuler, and his lady, Linda, were beautiful and gracious people. The ballroom there at the Muskogee Holiday Inn was dramatic with red balloon centerpieces, on round tables with red chairs, and tiny strings of bulbs provided romantic lights for the dance.

Klint was handsome in his western cut tuxedo, and I didn't go unnoticed either. I wore the diamond that was in the engagement ring he had given me on a tiny, gold, choker chain, and a flaming red, one-shoulder, sequined ball gown (borrowed from my sister, LaVoyce) was responsible for the title Sandy Williamson gave me: 'the lady in red'. Of all the people I met that weekend, Sandy was the one I remembered most. We enjoyed a fun conversation in the ladies restroom. Her many questions as to who and what I was to Klint, housed in a chummy familiarity, prompted me to tell her more than I had planned. She was to become a fan of mine, and as the years rolled on, she often cast asperities on Klint for 'letting me go'.

My flight back to my life in Flagstaff was a time spent with questions. I wondered why we had spent so little time that weekend talking about our current lives. I knew only that his mom lived with him in McAlester; that he filled his days and nights with Shriner and Scottish Rite involvements, and that he had been going with the same woman, off and on, for years. And, that was more than he knew about my life. I got the impression that he preferred it that way. The undeniable question, that was the elephant in the bed with us, was why? Why did we have such a connection? If nothing was to come of it, why? Obviously, the passage of time made no difference. Yet, he had made no move to address the puzzle our relationship continued to be. He gave no indication that he wanted me in his life at all. But how then could he make love to me the way he did, and not be the least bit invested in me? Sure, I had been the one to break up with him, but that was five years ago. You would think that a man, trained for hand to hand combat as a Ranger, and who was a member of the 82nd Airborne Division during World War II would be up to any challenge. So by the time I landed in Phoenix, all the thrill of being with him again was gone. A melancholy took its place and settled into my heart and stayed there all the way up the mountain to Flagstaff.

Now in the year 1995, as I was putting on fresh makeup, I felt a knot in my stomach and a stirring of my heart. I could predict the evening: high energy conversation that would feature his life, not mine; a rare steak dinner for me; a night of familiar and intimate love making, and then he would be gone again without a word about the mystery of us.

"Okay," I began, after we had ordered drinks, "Tell me how you got my phone number?"

Klint stretched back in his chair, tilted his head to one side as was his habit and answered me with a question. "Do you remember how I can sort of know things without there being any reason for me to?"

"Sure, I know your stories that are evidence of your extra-sensory perception. So?" I leaned forward, took a sip of my wine and smiled into his eyes.

"Well, it's like this" he smiled back, "I rolled into town around five o'clock today, got a room at the Best Western, and was gonna have a Bourbon and 7 before dinner. But, for some reason, I felt really nervous. I was plumb jittery. At first I just stalked around the room. Then I walked outside to get some air, but that didn't help either. So I went back inside, turned on the TV, but I couldn't make myself watch it. I then stormed back outside and that's when it hit me. I knew you were somewhere close around. I was so sure that I hurried over to my truck, got my address book out, and called your dad. He told me you were in Flagstaff working at NAU, and gave me your new phone number."

I sat for a moment and watched his face. Such confidence and a sprinkle of frolic in those faded blue eyes.

And of course I believed him. This was who Klint was - a mixture of the abstruse and the conspicuous. His willingness to share an experience that might be suspect, in spite of his need for approval, gave him credibility.

Everything was the same. He still shared his life history with the waitress; he still butchered the King's English; I still had to repeat most everything I said, and he still made me privy to unasked-for news about his current political views and all his state and national Shriner involvements. Klint was a one man show, and if it wasn't for the ardent way he made love to me, I might conclude that I was just this evening's audience. But no. His eyes betrayed him. He was still in love with me, but I'd probably never hear him say it again.

The morning sunshine had found its way into Denny's, and I was going to be late for work, but I knew my secretary Lana would be able to cover for me. I was reluctant to leave the breakfast table, so I kept accepting more coffee from the waitress.

"How about you coming to Oklahoma and going to the Potentate Ball with me?" Clint offered this invitation almost like he didn't want to, but couldn't help himself as he was getting up to pay the bill.

"Really?" Now this was something about me and I was interested. "Oh Klint, absolutely. You know how I love to dress up. If you can pay my way, I'll be there with bells on."

"You've got it," was his instant response. The way he could never hide his feelings made it clear to me that he was as enthused about the idea of being together again next month as I was. The only down side was that I was just excited about a fun and unexpected weekend trip, but I knew that his happy feelings were all about being with me. Guess it was a good thing we didn't really talk about anything that mattered.

And then there was Brian. I never knew which one of them, Klint or Brian, would be the evening's trip down memory lane. My weeknight ritual of swimming until

12

exhaustion, then watching the Houston sky as I floated in Cameron's pool until bedtime, gave them time to monopolize my reverie. The story of how Brian and I met in Flagstaff was one of my favorites.

My Honda, Shotsy, was in the driveway ditch, and the only way to get out of the car was to climb over the passenger's seat, crawl through the window, and tumble into the deep snow. "Damn", I mumbled, as I dusted the snow off my coat. I will never learn how to back a car. I hated feeling inept, but having to trudge through the knee-deep snow back into my warm house was evidence of it. As I dialed my office at NAU, I took a deep breath to prepare for what I knew would be my secretary Lana's thinly veiled irritation.

"Bonn, why don't you move to where it doesn't snow, because IF you could learn how to drive in Arizona you would have by now. You have lived here how many years? Five is it?" was Lana's response to my barely audible announcement that I would be late for work.

"I'm calling the only gas station here in Munds Park for a pull, and I will be there ASAP. That's all I can do, now that I am stuck. Please cover for me. I don't remember any appointments, but you better check my desk calendar to make sure." I hated my deserved driving reputation, and no doubt Lana would get plenty of mileage out of this latest episode at noon break.

The phone rang and rang and rang. Why in the world didn't the station guy answer? They were always open. But after the fourth try at staying on the line forever I gave up; put on all my snow gear once again, and opened the door into the garage. The sun was out and the new snow glistened, but it failed to lift my mood. Finally I got my snow boots on, and as I straightened up to adjust my hat I very clearly heard a voice say, "Chill out, Bonn and put a smile on your face. You are about to meet someone."

It was so real that I actually looked around the empty garage for the owner of the voice, but then as I started walking past Shotsy, there in the driveway buried in the snow, I pondered the message. I was not spooked by the possibility of communication from something not in a body. However, it seldom was my experience. Usually, I would get a needed answer via a thought that I credited to my guides, not unsolicited advice from a loud, clear actual voice.

There was no traffic, thus my plan to flag down the first car to come my way had to wait awhile. The deep snow kept my progress at a snail's pace, so I was ready, long before necessary, with my thumb up to hitch a ride from the silver truck slowly coming my way from the north. The good Samaritan slowed to a stop and I opened the door.

There he was! A smiling, ski-slope tanned, blond Greek god whose instant and welcoming greeting set the tone for familiar, easy, non-stop conversation all the way to the gas station. I silently cautioned myself not to forget one detail. There was something familiar about the man, but I didn't have time to think about it. This intrigue made it difficult to concentrate on what he was saying. He introduced himself, and I thoughtfully repeated his name so I would remember it. Brian Berwald. He lived there in Munds Park, and he was on his way to put his dog to sleep (doctor's orders). No mention of a wife or family. But when he said goodbye at the station, no mention of seeing each other again either!

As I watched the tow truck pull Shotsy out of the ditch and onto the waiting street, I struggled to decide which question to consider first. Was he old enough? With those sunglasses on there was no way to determine his approximate age. Why didn't he ask for my phone number? He seemed as interested as I was. Maybe that's it. Was I too obviously charmed? Because of his gloves, I couldn't see if there was a wedding ring on his finger. No doubt he had to be married.

Not having answers to my tumbling questions didn't diminish my emotional high. As I drove cautiously to Flagstaff, parked Shotsy, and rushed into my office in the

Center for Excellence, an uncanny conviction spilled forth to the first person I saw. "Lana, I've just met the man I am going to marry." Damn! Where in the hell did that come from? I felt like a fool, and Lana confirmed it.

"Oh please, Bonn. Aren't you ever going to grow up?" She rolled her eyes and dismissed me with, "You will find the list of phone messages you need to return on your desk."

As the days finally made a week, I was puzzled and disappointed that he hadn't called. After all, he knew my name and where I worked. That was enough information for anyone really interested, and I was sure he was. My intuition told me that he was as attracted to me, as I was to him. I was certain of that. So what was up? Never one to give the unknown too much of my time, after two weeks of waiting for his call, I finally dialed his phone number. I had looked it up the day we met.

"Hello, Brian? This is Bonn Ritland. Maybe you remember giving me a ride to the station a couple of weeks back. My car was stuck in the snow, and you saved the day." I was going for light and casual.

"Hey. Sure I remember. How's it going?"

I was relieved that he sounded glad to hear from me, but I intended to know immediately if he was married. "Is calling you appropriate?"

Brian laughed. "Yes, absolutely. I have been away on a skiing trip, and just got back yesterday. In fact, you were on my list of things to do today. Glad you've saved me search time. If you don't already have plans, want to meet me for a hamburger during your lunch break tomorrow?"

The weight of wondering was lifted immediately. He had been out of town; he was interested in me too, and most importantly, he was single. I was glad that I had risked calling him.

He was already there and waiting for me. As I walked slowly to the table, it was easy to see, for the first time, what the man really looked like. The mass of fine, blond curls was his most striking attribute, and framed an attractive face. Yet, if you considered each feature separately, not really. His eyes were blue, but even though they were larger than the norm, they still lacked strength. His nose was large and long with a very narrow beginning between his eyes, and high, permanently pink cheeks helped to keep one's attention from his oversized ears. Nevertheless, as I sat down across from him, I concluded that Brian would qualify as a trophy.

And, of course, he was taking me in too. Without my snow cap, bulky red coat and sunglasses, he had an unobstructed view of my 'had-been-blond-now-almost gray' thick, short hair; wide-set, large, blue eyes over high Cherokee Indian cheek bones, and as I slipped into the booth, he could see my tall, svelte body that was testimony to daily gym workouts. He extended his hand and said teasingly, "And how is the neighborhood snow bunny? I trust you have been staying in the ruts."

I couldn't even manage the expected hello. I knew I was smiling, but nothing would come out of my mouth. How could I have missed it? Or did I? Maybe, on a subconscious level, I had recognized him. Maybe that is why I had told Lana I had met the man I would marry. Brian was the spitting image of Josh Warrington, the student teacher I had gotten romantically involved with earlier this year. Josh, a past life regression in Sedona had identified as a husband in Cedar Grove, Louisiana in 1902. A man who had not loved or honored me, and I had felt that when I married him. Nevertheless, because I needed his love for validation of my worth, I had disregarded the obvious. Thus my years spent as his wife had been miserable. That life ended in Tibet, of all places. In the last scene of my life, I was 50 years old. No longer beautiful, but surrounded by people I felt connected to. My guide, during this past life regression, explained to me that the explosion of love that I felt for myself as I was dying was the lesson of that lifetime. He had said, "This loving yourself is the basis for the way you relate to everyone. You know it isn't the ego thing. It's not this 'I am so wonderful' attitude. It's the awareness of your higher self, and how you (as is everyone, whether they know it or not) are connected to the Power. All this knowingness then culminates into what love really is. For yourself, for others, for life."

Stop the flashback, I told myself. I was struggling to stay in the moment. The past was screaming for my attention, yet this demand for recognition made every detail of the present more vitally important. At last I could speak. Laughingly I said, "This snow bunny is still grateful for the neighborhood good Samaritan. But what's up with you going skiing and me going to work?"

Brian was like all the men I had ever known. They love to talk about themselves, consequently he began chatting away about his vacation in Colorado. I could smile, nod and appear to be listening while my mind was scrambling to make some sense of what was happening. I was cataloguing everything about him. The way he phrased his words, his body language, his habit of making a faint sniffing noise were all exactly like Josh. Brian was an older, taller, close physical replica of Josh, who had been in my life briefly but dramatically months earlier. He could be Josh's father because of how similar their mannerisms were. And Josh was the reincarnation of that cruel husband in Louisiana. Damn, I was spooked.

Good grief! Too much paranormal before lunch. Give it a rest, I was thinking, when I heard Brian say. "Actually, Bonn. I am married."

I was surprised, but not destroyed by this announcement. He didn't blink or hesitate to explain, "However, I have been considering not being for some time now."

As I sat there looking at him, I felt a small smile change my lips. I wasn't upset, disappointed or repulsed. And, the first thought that registered was, 'Good. Now I don't have to worry about getting involved with another man'. Yet, right on the heels of that was my memory of: 'You told Lana that you had met the man you are going to marry.'

Instantly, my discerning nature nailed my unwillingness to change my ways. Two contradictory thoughts in bed with each other. I can always see the red flags waving over a prospective relationship, yet at the same time, I mindlessly go too quickly right to another altar. Most people put a great deal of thought into marriage. But from the first time I married, to the last, not me. I went from blind date to wedding ceremony in two months time when I married the father of my children, and only six weeks from stranger to husband right after the divorce that ended my first marriage of 27 years, and then most recently, a one year marriage with an Arizona realtor in 2001, after only a summer of boating weekends on Lake Powell. So why in the world would I think for one minute that Brian being married would save me from myself?

"Well, my goodness!" I chuckled. "Actually, it's alright. If my oldest son were here, he'd tell you that I'm not marriage material anyway, so I don't see that we have a problem."

Brian was visibly relieved. "Well, like I said, this being married is soon to be history."

I looked at him for a long moment before saying, "Let's just enjoy the predictable first date conversation, and leave it at that. Tell me more about your life, I am a lover of biography."

Years later I would recall how Brian's attention to detail didn't irritate me during this first lunch. Funny how this habit of his would become so tedious for me. It is one of life's mysteries and a deadly one for relationships: with time, someone's personality can go from being endearing to intolerable. And the fact that he was more interested in his story than mine was not unexpected. Since deciding it was a guy thing, I no longer got irritated by it, but I always noticed it.

* * * * *

I had only been gone from Brian in Arizona for maybe two months when his call to ask if he could come see me on his way to Ohio to visit his mother and brother caught me by surprise. My thought was that Ohio, by way of Texas, spoke volumes.

Cameron didn't like Brian. I wasn't sure which of the several possible reasons she had chosen, but it was clear that she didn't like him. Her short, little body was stiff and unfriendly, and Brian didn't appreciate being put on the defensive. I watched them in her kitchen. The contrast between them was staggering. The long and the short of it. Brian towered over Cameron, but she was not intimidated by his height. She was angry at all men, and the fact that he was still married gave her all the ammunition she needed.

"So, do you plan on filing for divorce when you get back or do you still need more time to think about it?"

"I take it that you have been involved with a married man." Brian was smiling, but I suspected that his teeth were clenched.

"Of course. Hasn't everybody?" Her voice was ice, thus it seemed like a good time for me to call a halt to this verbal combat. I got up from the breakfast table saying,

"Okay you two. It's time to end this friendly chat. Brian? Are you ready to leave for Galveston? It will take us a couple of hours from this side of town."

He put his glass down like it was hot and turned on his heels. "You bet I am. Nothing like the beach to clear the air. Cameron, if I don't see you Sunday night when we get back, thanks for the overnight stay. You have a beautiful home."

"I love the way you two hit it off," I said, with a wicked smile, as Brian backed his camper pickup out of the driveway.

"Man. What a bitter woman. Is this her usual demeanor or have recent events done this to her?"

"Cameron is not her usual self these days, I can tell you for sure. The man she was married to is a total jerk, but the odd thing is she can't let it go. I honestly think she would take him back. Don't ask me why. I just get so tired of listening to all her complaints about him. She doesn't make up stuff, either. For sure he is awful, but if so, why does she keep stirring the pot? I advise her to let it go and so do all her friends. Nevertheless, she can't, yet. Sorry she was rude to you."

"Oh, that's okay. Actually, she has a point. Why haven't I filed for divorce? I think I told you the first time we had lunch together that I was working on it. That was six months ago. Time enough, don't you think?"

"No comment. I'm not going to be a party to that decision. It is your call, not mine. You have to know that I left Flagstaff and came back to Texas because it made financial sense to do so. However, that is not the whole story and you know that too. For four months you and I met secretly. Upstairs among book shelves of the university library; brief lunchtime picnics in the nearby woods during my work week; a hike one Saturday in the Sedona red rocks when your wife was out of town. Just because I didn't say anything doesn't mean that I didn't notice that you remained married. So, dear one, if a couple of nights in your camper on the beach is what you are about, that works for me. After all, I live in Texas now and you are still in Arizona. Not likely that we will run into each other at the grocery store. You know I am thrilled to be with you; that I am loving this weekend with you; that I have missed you, but hey, those facts don't qualify me to become a part of your decision making about your life. It is strictly your call."

I wish my cavalier attitude had survived the weekend. It was beyond wonderful to sleep with Brian there on the beach in his camper. Becoming sexually intimate probably wasn't the best idea for maintaining the 'you decide, it is your life' line. By Sunday night when he left I was in a heap. The Monday morning scary government classroom was looming, plus his driving off towards Ohio to visit his mother and brother, about did me in. And my premonition that the coming week would be awful was right. Doing laps in the pool to the point of exhaustion didn't help as much as they had in the past. The only saving grace was having to listen to Cameron's ongoing trauma drama. It kept my mind off my own.

It had been a long time since I had taught seniors, and I had forgotten how wonderful they can be. Seldom, if ever, did I have to correct their behavior. If only I felt confident as their government teacher, all would have been just fine. However, I absolutely could not get my arms around the subject matter. I had always loved teaching history because it is just one story after another. But I could not figure out how to make the judicial, legislative or executive branches of government interesting. Consequently, I spent much more time than I ever had preparing lesson plans. Even so, I never walked out to my car at the end of the day with the good feeling of accomplishment. This was a new experience for me, and one I hated. I had always taken so much pleasure in being an outstanding teacher. But now, I wasn't even a good one. Where, in my life now, was some joy? My dad was fighting cancer; my love life was a combo of two impossible, distant men; my credit card debt was sky high, and living at Cameron's was the icing on my miserable cake. The weekend my two granddaughters spent with me was validation that it was time to do whatever it took to get some happiness back into my life. Enter, my granddaughters from rural South Texas.

I called them my sunshine girls. Megan was six now and Cody was close behind at four. Both girls were very tall, tanned, slim, blond, and beautiful. Cameron's pool was their favorite place to play, and I think it was Megs who named the automatic pool cleaner Oscar. They both treated this machine like it was a monster after them. Such splashing, yelling, running and jumping! I kept my eyes on them every minute because it didn't do any good to caution them not to get hurt. When I realized that neither of them would go in the house to get yet another soda, I would have them get out of the pool while I went to get them something cold to drink. I couldn't understand their refusal to go into the house alone. Cameron was gone, but she had been so sweet and welcoming to them. Actually, at first it aggravated me that they wouldn't mind me. They had never done that before, and it was such a simple, quick thing. Walk through the utility room into the kitchen, open the refrigerator and select a cold soda. I didn't see a problem, but both of them flatly refused to do it.

I ordered pizza and we ate it on the patio. It was getting to be sundown, and like the sun, the sunshine girls were about gone too. A shower, a video of their choice, and then bedtime was the plan. Megs wanted to take a bubble bath in Cameron's big tub, but Cody only wanted a quick shower. So I sent Cody on upstairs to shower, while I stayed with Megs because she was in Cameron's bathroom.

"Why is Miss Cameron so sad?" Megs was looking at a large picture painted in various shades of blue, of a solitary woman looking out to sea.

"What makes you think Miss Cameron is sad, Megs?"

Megs turned away from the picture and looked at me very seriously. "She is like that lady in the picture, very unhappy and about to cry".

Out of the mouth of babes, for sure, was my thought. Then, I aged ten years when I heard Cody scream. We met on the stairs. She was scrambling down and I was bounding up. She was white as a sheet. She threw herself into my arms and I held her tightly to stop her shaking.

"Cody? What on earth?"

She raised her head up from my chest and looked me right in the eyes. "Gran, the long black thing came out of your bedroom and started towards me."

"Cody, what in the world are you talking about? What black thing?"

She stood up straight and didn't blink an eye. "Gran, it was sort of filmy and close to the floor. It moved like a snake in water and it was coming at me. And, just never mind saying anything about it, I won't go back up there by myself".

"Sweetie, good grief. I am not going to make you go back up there. Come on, you can jump in the tub with Megs. I'll go get your jammies and then we can watch the video here in Miss Cameron's living room."

Instantly she was back to her high energy self. I got them settled into the tub before I walked up the stairs alone. I wasn't relaxed. I found myself looking along the baseboards of the sitting room, then my bedroom where Cody's clothes were. I knew she had seen something paranormal. It often happens with children, so I didn't question it at all. And all the stuff, beautiful stuff, but so much of it everywhere, had its usual effect on me. I felt like I couldn't breathe, so I rushed to get back down the stairs.

The weekend with the sunshine girls was over, and after my daughter picked up Megs and Cody, I was not all that comfortable with the thought of being upstairs. Now, adding to my claustrophobia, was the fear around something paranormal waiting for me. And sure enough, that night I had my first experience with some entity outside a body. I wasn't yet asleep. I had shut the door to my bedroom, and was settling into my bed when, from the ceiling, a large, threatening, black something rushed at me. I was so terrified that all the breath in my body left me. I closed my eyes, covered my head, and expected to die. Instead, there was silence and nothing. I lay without breathing and waited. Nothing! It was gone. I didn't turn on a light or move. I didn't think or cry. I was paralyzed in place, and it was a long time before I slept.

The next day was the familiar Monday, made worse because I was exhausted from the terrors of the night before. Consequently, stopping to listen to Cameron was last on my list as I walked through the living room headed for the stairs. I kept moving and all I said was hello. She was sitting on the couch and I could tell by the look on her face that things were worse than usual. She saw her ex-husband daily because they worked at the same high school, so it wasn't unusual that Cameron would have some story to add to the ongoing saga. But today I stopped her with a wave of my hand, and the excuse that I had to do my TM (transcendental meditation) upstairs. I didn't stop to look at her reaction, but from the stairs I said, "I'll be down in about 30 minutes."

The next thing I knew, Cameron was on the stairs screaming at me. In all the years we had been friends, we had never had a fight, so you can just imagine my shock at this hysteria directed at me. What she actually said didn't register at all. What I felt was pure horror at being subjected to such fury. I remained immobile even after I heard the back door slam and her car start. Slowly I sat down on the couch; closed my eyes, and began running my mantra in my head. Moments passed before my breathing settled and I was able to escape into my habitual meditation space. The answer I got was: 'It is time to find your own apartment.'

CHAPTER TWO

Winter, 1995 – June, 1996

'Solitary Life Is Best. Will I Remember That?'

There is something about living alone that satisfies my soul. Even if there is trauma, as in my failed attempt to be a good government teacher, I always find the peace I need in the space of the solitary life. And, the good news is that I found the perfect apartment on Cypresswood Drive, not far from Cameron's house. Meg's mom, Summer, drove to Houston to help me decide on the two bedroom, two bath, ground floor with a winding path from the large, covered patio through the tall pine trees to the huge, usually empty swimming pool. I didn't have any of my furniture, except for a mattress that Summer brought me from Ehler's Furniture in Hallettsville. I had left the few things I owned at my ex-housemate Clark's house in Sedona. Some day, some way, I would have to go after them. Wonder how that would happen, was my thought, as I put the sheets on the mattress that was on the floor of my new bedroom. I had my too many clothes in the wonderful mirrored closet in the master bath, and I had the essential dishes on loan from Summer. The empty living room, dining room, and second bedroom didn't depress me at all.

The patio was furnished with a colorful area rug, wicker chairs and table. Beautiful artificial plants, (I can't grow anything), that drew in the woodsy, green world surrounding me, were the finishing touches. The warm weather in

Houston allowed for time spent out there, even into late fall. If I could just make myself not smoke the two cigarettes (one with a glass of wine after school and the other after dinner), my life would have been exactly what I wanted. My daily habit at Cameron's of rehashing the Klint and Brian memories was waning too. Texas was beginning to get and keep my full attention. I was gravitating back to my distant past. I was absorbed once again with the family and friends I had left behind in 1990 when I moved to Sedona, AZ. The known in the places and people felt comforting to me. I was gathering myself back from Klint and Brian. Neither of them were a good idea for my life. Men, who just by their daily presence, would lure me away from myself. Strange how that was for me. Whenever I am single, ever so gradually I have a natural tendency toward marriage again. Yet, after I am married, the constant companionship takes me away from myself. I do it voluntarily. I take on the roles of domestic chief, social chairman and pleaser. At the same time, I accumulate a list of 'they should be this and not that'. Then, invariably with time, I fault them for the deceitful person I become. Add to all that the fact that in my heart I feel spiritually superior to them, and there you have it. Divorce material. As I sat on my patio watching the tall pine trees sway in the evening breeze, I couldn't help but wonder how long it would be before I got involved again. It helped that Klint and Brian were geographically unavailable, but what about Houston's huge male population? However, as it happened, there wasn't any need for someone new. The father of my children was enough company for me these days.

Reagh and I had remained friends after the divorce that ended our 27 year marriage. Friends, as in holiday gatherings at the ranch; his trip to Sedona to visit me and our son Lyle, and a Saturday night dinner and dance date whenever I was around, and he wasn't dating someone special. In some ways it felt like it always had. Being personal and close was something we had never been able to create during those many years of marriage. We were more like partners, each with our own duties and responsibilities for the family unit. It worked for us that way for almost twenty years. Our differences we kept under raps. Reagh's philosophy was, 'If you don't talk about it, it isn't happening.' He didn't share my adventurous spirit, and he felt threatened by my unorthodox ideas. Reagh wasn't and had never been a dedicated Lutheran, yet at the same time, he was not comfortable with my interest in New Thought. He hated his shift work for Mobil Oil and often lamented the fact that he couldn't afford to retire to ranching, yet he was incredulous at my suggestion that we sell out, move to Australia, and start a new life. We were polite and obliging parents and partners during the last seven years of our marriage. Me blaming him and my life there in that rural community for my depression, and him being so confused as to why I was so heavyhearted. Now, after our divorce, it seemed harmless enough to allow our lives to bump into each other occasionally. 'Reagh is safe', was my thought as I locked the patio door for the night. A girl needs a good dance partner once in a while, and we do have our children in common. Maybe he will keep me out of any temptation to get seriously involved with another man. These things were on my mind as Thanksgiving approached.

Reagh's family was large and local. Holidays always brought them together, thus the plan to have the traditional turkey dinner at his house was expected and all accepted the invitation. The fact that I was playing hostess didn't appear to bother anyone. It was a cool fall day, so the herd of children could run inside and out. Megan, with Cody as her co-pilot, was clearly the leader. She directed the playing and was in charge of 'what we do next'. Megs always had her eye on 'what was next'. Summer had often commented, "She is just like you, Mother. The moment may be wonderful, but part of her brain is considering what comes after this." And, the way my daughter always made this observation left no doubt that she didn't see this common characteristic as a plus.

I tried to comfort her with my usual, "Yes, my blood is half gasoline, just like my daddy's. And did that ruin his life? I don't think so. Megs, unlike you, won't live and die in this one Texas town, and how bad can that be?" Summer was as content and constant in her life, as I was wandering and wanting in mine. Thank goodness this difference worked for us. I took comfort in her stability, and I suspected that she lived vicariously through my adventures.

I don't really remember when it became a tradition for me to say the Thanksgiving and Christmas dinner blessings whenever those holidays were celebrated at the ranch house. But somehow, the divorce hadn't ended it. I put as much thought into the prepared prayer as I did the turkey and dressing. This year was no different. Everyone gathered in the large dining room, held hands, and I read:

"This Thanksgiving Day we pause to bless the winds of change. Those winds that blow and redesign our lives. Do we resist their might or gladly bend? Either way - they come to alter the multitude of plans the mind contrives.

"The cutting wind of change sweeps from us our life's design, and leaves us cleansed to comprehend the tender breeze that follows as friend to comfort us - that breeze from which love derives. And though we may be wishing softer winds today - those that don't pierce our souls - help us, God, to remember while we bear the chilling blast, that some sweeter, healing breath will come at last.

"Help us, this day of thanksgiving because we tend to forget. That it is our spirit that travels these winds of change. For within us there is a long forgotten dream they carry us to. A dream in which we remember our true heritage in the Light. Thus, we can choose to be thankful, for how fierce they blow or soft they sigh. Because change is the vehicle, the route, the way, to the light of the Christ within."

I don't know why I put so much thought into writing the blessing, year after year. It was always met with a very loud silence. I never knew if they just didn't get what I was saying, or they were so shocked at my ideas that they couldn't utter a word. Even before we were divorced, I was experienced by Reagh's family as divergent in my way of thinking. They all loved me, that I was sure of. Too, they enjoyed hearing about my escapades. My high school classroom stories were famous for the hilarious happenings and the unprecedented community reaction to my world history lessons. I guess the real deal was that, as a group, they couldn't get their arms around how Reagh and I were living our divorce. Our roles as husband and wife had ended, but we were not enemies. We still loved and respected each other. We actually could now enjoy each other's company much more because we no longer had anything invested in who the other one was. We could feed cows together, sleep together, go dancing together, and not know or even care what the other one was thinking. As I drove back to Houston after any particular holiday weekend, I thought about how that might be the problem with marriage. When you live with someone, how they think, what they want, what they do, really impacts your life. However, when they are only the icing on your cake, as in weekend and special occasions togetherness, then you stand a better chance of being happy on a more consistent basis. That is, if you are healthy, enjoy a meaningful career, and are financially independent. Let's hope that I remember this, was my thought as I got out of Shotsy, my red Honda Civic, and walked to unlock the door to my wonderful Houston apartment.

I had been a member of the Unity Church of Christianity in Houston in the 1980's, and I looked forward to attending it again. I could depend on the message being inspiring and directed at my needs, and lunch with a lady friend at Houston's Restaurant there close to the Gallaria was the highlight of Sunday. My association with the church was a Sunday- only thing because it was too far to drive to during the week for special classes. Therefore, I found another Unity church close to my apartment. It had been a private home; it was in the middle of five acres of pine trees, and the congregation was small and welcoming. And, as always, when I am single and live alone, I turn inward. My spiritual life directs my external one. I enroll in every personal growth course offered, I tithe my limited money, I keep gratitude journals, I read all the recommended books by the popular gurus, and I attempt to make each day a walking prayer. And it is obvious to me, as I write and then recite my always increasing list of affirmations, that my need for more money, (whenever I am single), is a constant in my life. I could almost say them from memory.

"I am the Spirit of Infinite Plenty individualized. I am boundless abundance in radiant expression. What is expressed in love must be returned in full measure. Therefore, wave after wave of visible money supply flows to me now."

"I am wonderfully rich in consciousness. I now realize my plan for abundant living. I happily see every bill paid now. I see my bank account continually filled with an all-sufficiency to meet every need with a Divine surplus. I see myself sharing this bounty for the good of all. With great delight, I see the continuing flow of this money used with love and wisdom as I create the perfect scenes according to my highest vision."

"I cast this burden of financial debt on the Christ within, and I go free."

"All financial obligations are now wiped out under grace in a miraculous way."

Additionally, the process in the prosperity course had me following an exact plan of action:

1. Create a vacuum by saying, "I fully and freely release. I loose and let go. I joyously make way for

my new good, which now appears quickly in satisfying and appropriate form."

2. Get definite about what I want. "This or something better, Father. Let Thy highest good now manifest. Let the divine result now appear."

3. Mentally picture the good. Affirm: "This or something better, Father. Let Thy highest good now manifest. Let the divine result now appear in the divine way."

4. Speak daily affirmations: "My world is the perfect creation of divine substance. The finished results of divine substance now appear as peace, health, and plenty in my world."

5. Think of myself as already prosperous. "Divine substance is the one and only reality. Therefore, I have plenty of everything now."

It would be many, many years before I would look back at this solitary time spent in the woods around this church and ask myself if my absorbing pursuit of what I thought of as my spiritual path wasn't paved with financial need. If so, does that mean that experiencing oneself as a spiritual being who can direct their life circumstances, delusional? Being a student of myself has always generated more questions than answers.

How to get my furniture, computer, and dishes from Clark's house in Sedona was answered by my daughter-in-law. Cody's mom wanted to go see her mother in Prescott, AZ, and she would be pulling a trailer because she too was to collect a piece or two of furniture. There was room for me and the need for my financial help with the trip. Therefore, the Christmas season started with our trip west on Interstate 10.

Cody was the easiest child I had ever been around. Unlike Megan, she didn't require continual variety. Her first years had been spent playing with toys in her playpen under the large tree's shade by the horse barn. Her mom would train horses nearby, and Cody would play alone. There were family members who thought that this constituted child abuse, and others who saw it as typical of the Native American way. Whatever it was, the end result for Cody was that she became a child who was very comfortable with solitude. Yet at the same time she was a most loving and affectionate child. Megs was her favorite person. She always referred to her as 'my cousin'. Whether they were riding across the pasture in Megs' pink jeep, going to a musical at the Alley Theatre dressed in their finest; winning the Halloween Contest as a Dallas Cowboy Cheerleader and a bride, or playing in the apartment swimming pool, Cody rivaled Megs for gregariousness. Nevertheless, as we drove west on Interstate 10 towards Sedona, she never let out a peep. No demand for interaction from her mother or me. She was stuffed in the back seat of the pickup content with all her books and toys for mile after mile.

I was very disappointed to find that my favorite lounge chair was ruined because of Clark's dog peeing on it. Too, all my china and crystal were no longer in the garage. There had been a garage sale, and mine was mistakenly sold. Did I believe that? Clark was someone I had trusted completely, however, there was a new roommate who may have been responsible. Bottom line, I didn't have much to load when it was time to go. Only my desk, computer, dishes and cooking pans, pictures and lamps, and the bed frame for my new mattress. Not much in the way of worldly possessions. I would have to use my credit card again to purchase furniture in Houston. Why bother trying to pay it off. Seems there is always some giant need that runs it back up once more.

The drive back to Texas was long. My daughter-in-law didn't talk much, but what little she did say validated my suspicions that she and Jon were not doing well. Her life as a child and young woman had been unhappy and traumatic, and that sad reality had left its mark on her psyche. Her inclination was to be mistrustful of people. She wasn't comfortable in a crowd. Yet somehow, even with limited interaction with society, she had managed to form dogmatic opinions about many things. Maybe that was the result of much reading and obvious intelligence. She was wrapped in melancholy and wasn't up for small talk as she drove the truck towards Texas.

When we stopped in Fort Stockton for dinner, I heard Cody whine for the first time ever. It was cold and I stood in the door of the truck trying to get shoes on her fat little feet. Her blond long curls were a mess and she looked at me with sad eyes and said, "Gran, my body hurts sooooo bad." I told her mom and we decided to let Cody run and play while we ate our meal. The other customers were happy to give her encouragement; the huge fireplace was a fascination to her, and the room was large enough for her to get the much needed exercise. After we got back into the truck to continue down Interstate 10, she ate her boxed dinner and then went sound to sleep.

I was dead tired by the time we got to Houston, and while Jon, my oldest son, quickly unloaded my few possessions, I was tempted to cancel my plan to drive on to Nacogdoches to spend Christmas with my parents. I didn't, however, thinking 'How hard can it be to drive another three hours'. Wrong! I could hardly keep the car in the road. I was so sleepy that I kept having to pull off the road and walk around the car in the cold wind to wake up. When I stopped to get a hamburger, I was crossing a busy street when I misjudged an approaching car, thus I came within inches of being hit. I could feel the hot air of the car on my face. I took the few steps to get off the highway and then collapsed to the ground. The driver stopped and helped me up. He was almost as upset as I was. The only plus of the incident was it scared me so badly, that I didn't have any more trouble staying awake for the rest of the drive to Nacogdoches.

I was glad that I had made the effort to get to Daddy. He was so glad to see me and I slept like the dead on their living room couch. The plan was to drive over to his sister's house for Christmas dinner the next day. It was a beautiful drive through the East Texas woods, and there was a large crowd gathered. My dad loved his family and everyone loved him too. And, as always, Mother was the most beautiful woman there (even in her 70's), and the coldest. Her lack of regard for 'the Joneses', as she always called them, was a given with her. Everyone just seemed to accept and expect her to sit in their presence like royalty and dare anyone to talk to her. Long before Daddy wanted to leave, she announced that we were going. As always, he got his coat and left without objection. As we drove back to Doches in silence, I felt the old terror rise up in my throat. I was like my mother in so many ways. I looked like her; I had some of the same mannerisms; my fault finding with a husband, and my never being completely happy with whatever life I was living. Then, remembering that one creates their reality by the way they think, I tried to comfort myself and stop the fear with the thought that in many ways I was not my mother. I did love my children and showed it; I did understand that I wasn't a victim, and I did take an interest in other people. Nevertheless, the book, *My Mother, Myself*, came to mind, and it made me shiver.

New Year's Eve is party night. I had always insisted on partying regardless of where I was in the world. Therefore, Reagh's invitation to come to the ranch and go with him to a dinner/dance in La Grange had me dancing around my apartment and searching my closet for the perfect cocktail dress. I could look forward to a happy festive evening with no strings attached. I really could have a good time with him because he was the best dancer in all of Texas; he was good looking and always dressed stylishly, and he would be in a good mood. No worries about what he might do or say that would upset me. No worries about the future of our relationship. It had all been decided. We were divorced. Our marriage was history. If he was still hurt and disappointed in me it didn't show. He was the most eligible bachelor in Lavaca County, so his social calendar was always full. No. Our times together were now all about enjoying the moment at hand. So I danced my way into 1996 with a smile on my face, and in the arms of the father of my children.

The first good news of 1996 came from my principal at Eisenhower High School. I was being moved from teaching government to American history. Glory hallelujah! Answer to my daily affirmations for accomplishment and success in my classroom. I would now be able to work my magic with sophomores and feel like I had earned my paycheck each month. I was fairly walking on Cloud 9 as I designed new bulletin boards. The students would be harder to manage, but with my experience in teaching history, I'd earn their cooperation. I always had. Why should this time be any different? And it wasn't. Driving home now to my apartment, the Houston traffic didn't even upset me. Life was good. Really good. Time to take on another project.

When I was Student Teacher Coordinator at NAU I was earning my master's degree in Educational Leadership. I had only six hours left when I moved back to Houston. Therefore, it made sense to finish that degree, thus driving the thirty or so miles to Prairie View A&M University every Wednesday night and Saturday morning from January to May was the thing for me to do. I always enjoyed taking college courses, and this was no different. Actually, it was a piece of cake. No exams, only papers to write and presentations to give. My cup of tea. Two Saturdays a month, I would drive on over to Nacogdoches to spend the night with Mom and Dad. My life developed into an unchanging pattern. Attend Saturday's class, pick up some Church's Fried Chicken and then stop at one particular roadside park and have a solitary picnic. The country roads were never boring to me, and I would always arrive mid afternoon for time with Daddy before we drove to his favorite catfish place for dinner. My life now had a rhythm to it that left little room for new people or places. I taught school all week; I read at night; I went to school and did homework; I visited my parents almost every weekend; I attended the Unity church near my apartment; I joined my friend, Charlye Jo, for a weekly meditation; I drove to Hallettsville to see my family and maybe go dancing with Reagh, and I worked out five days a week at the apartment gym. Nothing but the same routine, week after week. I felt grounded and secure. It didn't last. Why did I think it would?

It was a package and letter from Brian that began the next saga of my life. He sent me two wonderful, framed photos of northern Arizona. His letter told me about his travels, solo and sometimes with his mom. The photos were evidence of his talent for photography and his plan to make it a paying hobby in the future. And, oh yes: he misses me, and he has filed for divorce, and he wants to move to Houston and live with me. As I stare at the letter I experience instant elation and turmoil, all wrapped together in 'could this be next?' Now I have a whole new inner dialogue that runs as I exercise, sit on my patio smoking more than one cigarette, and drive to and from Hallettsville and Nacogdoches. All this, as I am editing my book, *Higher Ground, One Woman's Journey*. Relationship circles, past and present, is a tape constantly running in my head, even at school when I am trying to lecture about the causes of the Civil War.

So then the phone calls begin, and the weekly letters come from Brian. He can talk and write forever. Such detail to every aspect of our possible future. He will get a teaching job in Houston so we will have the same holidays and summers off; we can buy a home together; we can move to Mexico or Costa Rico when I retire in four years, and no mention of getting married. As the weeks went from the last of winter to the beginnings of spring, it was sounding better and better to me. Maybe I could have my cake and eat it too this time. We would not be married, but I would have the pleasure of his company and the benefit of his financial involvement in my life.

The 'possibility of Brian' became one of my favorite topics to probe during the weekly meditation with Charlye Jo and a few new friends. The house where we met was very opulent, and I loved its effect on me. The weeks were moving quickly toward the end of May when school would be out. Brian was waiting for my answer. Then, a more immediate and financial crisis developed during the last couple of weeks of school.

The memo read: All teachers are responsible for textbooks issued to their students. This announcement from the principal only made me mildly concerned until I asked my students to give me their book numbers. Among the correct responses was added: "I don't know where my book is." "I'll bring it tomorrow." "I never got a book." "Joe has it, so he will give it to you." My growing panic and daily reminders didn't change a thing. There were now only two weeks left, and my figures showed that I was missing twenty three books. At the rate of thirty five dollars a book, that meant that I would owe the Altair Independent School District eight hundred and five dollars. Might as well been a million because there was no way I could put my hands on that much money.

My meditation group got involved. With Charlye Jo as the voice, we affirmed the appearance of the texts, and I prayed daily for some miracle. Every morning before I did my Transcendental Meditation, I would visualize me being so happy because I had all the books. Nevertheless, I must not have really expected it to work because when it did, I almost died of shock. I couldn't help but notice that all the while I am saying affirmations, visualizing a happy outcome, and operating on the theory that everything is energy, and I have control over how my thoughts add to it, I can then still be surprised when I get what I want.

It happened in bits and pieces. First, the assistant principal walked into my classroom with a cart filled with textbooks. Ten of them were mine. Then one of the other history teachers left two of my books in my mailbox in the teacher's lounge. During lunch, the teacher who was on hall duty stopped by my room to deliver three more. After school I decided to turn in the ones I had and to continue to hope I would find the ones yet missing. The teachers had a workday the next day and my plan was to go from room to room in search of the last books needed. As I was standing in line waiting my turn, a teacher I didn't know handed me a book she thought was mine. It was. When I gave the textbook person my name, she said, "Wait a minute. I think I have some of your books here. Yes, I have six."

As I slowly stumbled back toward my room, I fairly weaved down the hall. My mind was spinning. I'm saved. The affirmations worked. Only one book missing. I could pay for one book. Hell, I was happy to pay for one book. I must have been in a state of shock, because the principal had to call again to get my attention. "Bonn. I have one of your books. The counselor said it was left in the detention hall." Now, who says we aren't powerful creatures who can impact our reality with our minds? Yet, it strikes me as bizarre that our lives should be so tough when we are all so brilliant. What a story to tell. I couldn't wait to report to my meditation group and to thank them for their help.

First, I called Cameron to tell her the good news. Now that nine months had passed since I moved out of her haunted house, memory of that deluge of fury from her tortured soul had been almost erased. We started going to movies together and sometimes we would go to dinner during the week. Not that the subject of conversation had changed much. Her ex-husband lived in my apartment complex and she was still interested in his every move. However, being around her was more bearable for me. It wasn't the same as living with her and being a captive audience. I could escape to my apartment. Nevertheless, I would then spend the rest of the evening trying not to be angry at her for being such an idiot. I knew that my thoughts about how this condition of 'being in love' made such fools of people wasn't good for my soul. I knew I was too prone to find fault with people, and I didn't want to do that. And, Cameron wasn't the only woman I knew who excused their ridiculous behavior with that reason. Being in love was a feeling that was subject to change, like all else in life. I knew more than one woman who had a problem with that reality, but not me. I certainly was in love with Reagh when we married. Now, I just loved him. Different yes, but freeing. Cameron wouldn't let it go. She was driving herself and all her friends crazy.

"Bonn, glad you called," was Cameron's opening comment. "I saw my principal at lunch today and she told me that her friend, the principal at the Alternative Learning Center, was looking for a history teacher for next year. I gave her your name. Knowing your addiction to change, I thought you might be interested."

"What's the Alternative Learning Center?" I decided to ignore her little dig. Besides, it was true.

"It is a school with a small population where all the students in the Cypress Fairbanks ISD are sentenced for wrong doing. They have to work their way out with good behavior and passing grades. You get combat pay, but I don't know how much it is. The school is closer too than Eisenhower."

Something new. A chance to make more money. Different students with special needs. Smaller classes. Before I said a word, I knew I would apply. Two days later I did. As I walked into the front door of the empty school, I knew I would get the job. I did.

CHAPTER THREE

June, July, August, 1996

'Summer Vacation and Brian'

I was sitting on the patio waiting for Brian, and I was not smoking. That would be another perk to having him come live with me. He didn't smoke, so I certainly would not. It was mid- afternoon when he pulled up in his rèd and black Mazda convertible. It was already hot in Houston, thus his face was flushed with the heat because instead of having the air conditioner on, he had the top down. I was to learn that one of the things on his hate list was cold weather. His body temperature ran cold all year. Guess it was because his blood had so far to go to make the round trip. I had almost forgotten how tall he was until we were walking through the pine trees to the pool. We had it to ourselves and that was a good thing because he couldn't keep his hands off me.

Beginnings are so incredible! The homefront was perfect. He had his own bathroom. There was a closet for his clothes, so I didn't have to share mine. He too was very neat and organized. My new living room furniture was comfortable for him, and he knew his way around the kitchen too. Happily, we loved doing the same things. On some weekends we would drive to Galveston for a day on the beach. During the week we would go to Barnes & Noble on Highway 1960 and spend hours reading about Belize, Mexico, and Costa Rico. He, like me, was always interested in the next place and life. He was more traveled than me, and I enjoyed his stories about Europe especially.

During these ideal weeks together there was one red flag. Just a day or two after Brian moved in, we went grocery shopping together for the first time. His propensity for detail and perfection showed itself in the almost two hours we spent selecting food. He would read one label, then another, and then compare the prices. Following that process, he would ask for my preference before putting the much examined item in the cart. Nine times out of ten I didn't care. After selecting a cart full of groceries, we decided to go into the video section of the Kroger Mega Store and get a couple of movies before checking out. While we were deciding on movies, some clerk must have determined that our grocery cart had just been abandoned and it was in the process of being emptied when we realized what had happened. Sure I was exasperated, but I didn't explode. However, Brian was infuriated, and he was so vocal about it that the store manager had a hard time calming him down. No one else could do the shopping again for us, so we had to. Sure, the store discounted the cost for our trouble, but I wasn't thinking about the time or money spent. My head hurt so badly that I was sick to my stomach, and memories of life with an explosive mother completely took me over. The minute we got in the car I turned to Brian and said, "I can't live with anyone who has such an uncontrollable temper."

His reaction took me by surprise. It was like what had just happened was a minor inconvenience that he hardly recalled. He smiled at me and started the car. It was hot as hell in Shotsy because she had been sitting in the sun for hours. I was totally upset and he was as cool and calm as I had ever seen him.

"Oh, I'm sorry. That was some deal, huh?" His nonchalance amazed me. Clearly he was past the event and not in the least repentant. And, would you believe, I let it go. I didn't say another word. As we were putting away the groceries in our kitchen, I only made one more reference to what had happened.

"From now on, Brian-The-Bomb, I will do our grocery shopping solo."

How in the world had he gotten all that camping gear in that little Mazda? Actually, how did he get his six foot five inches of body in it? Consequently, my Honda Civic, Shotsy, became our travel car. And, we did a lot of traveling. Brian, like me, considered the summer months meant for vacation travel. Both being teachers, this had been our common experience.

Our major trip of the summer started with us driving west. Brian's favorite part of the country were the western states: California, Arizona, New Mexico. So off we went to enjoy a camping vacation in New Mexico. I had done very little camping in my life, but since Brian was the expert and we were so in love, how bad could it be?

Brian chose our destination for two reasons: he had researched the area and felt confident that it was a place we would enjoy, and I didn't have an opinion about possible locales. I was happy as a duck riding down the highway and having Brian as my tour guide. His interest in the details of a place soon became apparent. By the time we arrived at the campsite, I too was educated about the Nacimiento Mountains. For starters the name was Spanish for 'source of a river'. They are just west of the more prominent Jemez Mountains near the town of Cuba, and are separated from them by the Rio Guadalupe and the Rio de Las Vacas. According to Brian, the Nacimientos are of some geological interest despite their modest elevation, as they form the western boundary of the Rio Grande Rift, a major rift valley containing the Rio Grande River. Much of the range is within the San Pedro Parks Wilderness Area and is protected against development. Hiking trails crisscross the wilderness area, making it a popular destination for backpackers. It doesn't boast any great natural landmarks. It is just a large area of mostly undisturbed forested wilderness with rocky peaks, meadows, mountain streams, lakes and waterfalls, and only occasional houses and villages. Its more unusual features result from past volcanic activity. There are hot springs, sulfurous vents and a caldera - a ring of hills comprising the remains of several long-extinct volcanoes. Now, this geography lesson didn't exactly fit in my 'need-to-know' book, but it didn't bother me to listen to Brian talk about our destination. What did bother me was how long it took him to select a campsite.

Naturally, I was thinking ahead to dinner preparations on a camp stove. That, and the fact that it was getting to the end of the afternoon when we drove into the camp area, prompted me to finally demand to know what was taking so long. Brian would walk a site; stand and stare at it, move some rocks and leaves around, and then he would walk to another one and repeat this process. I don't know if it was my question or the tone of my voice, but it seemed to startle him.

"Brian, what *ARE* you doing?"

"Bonn, I have to find a spot for the tent that is flat as possible, and without roots or rocks that will make sleeping on the ground uncomfortable for us."

"Fine. I'll help. Just sitting here on this picnic table watching you is driving me crazy," I said as I got up to walk toward him. "I don't want to cook dinner in the dark."

With my involvement, we quickly settled on a site that was within close walking distance to the bathroom. His attention to detail and need for perfection I noticed, but it didn't distress me that summer day. Wish it hadn't years later. Why is it that habits or ways of being aren't sources of irritation at the beginning of a relationship, but as the years go by, they can become good reasons for divorce? Feels like a setup.

Thank goodness, I found that I really did enjoy camping. Sure it took longer to cook dinner, but with wine to drink as I did so, not a problem. Too, I was encouraged to discover that Brian's sleep mattress was really almost as good as a bed. The night sounds added to the adventure too. There was nothing between me and the night critters except a tent, but I was not one bit afraid. Brian was big and strong and right there. It was hard to decide what I enjoyed the most- the days of hiking and the hot springs or the nights of love-making with this new man. The whole package made for a lifetime of memories. And, for sure, our daily bathing in the hot springs won the prize.

This was another first for me, and the only thing I was armed with was all the information via Brian about hot springs. I was not prepared for the torturous walk over rocks and around fallen limbs while always climbing higher and higher. However, knowing what a physical treat lay in store for me, gave me the stamina to climb until I got there.

Over breakfast, Brian had educated me about these natural features resulting when ground water, heated by geothermal forces, is brought to the surface, typically becoming diluted with cool surface water on the way. He assured me that for the hot-spring aficionado, the greatest pleasure comes not from just looking at the spring, but from getting into the water for its therapeutic powers, not to mention just because it feels good - really good.

I also learned that there are two kinds of springs: developed and wild. We were going to experience the wild kind. I was told not to expect any creature comforts. I would have to sit on a rock at water's edge to doff my clothes, and pre-entry showers are pretty well out of the question, let alone amenities like poolside drinks that a developed spring may offer. On the other hand, he added with a smile, wild springs are generally open-air and take you 'back to nature' in ways that a developed spring may not. However, he warned, at a wild spring the water temperature is purely on an as-is basis. It might be too hot to stand in one pool, but tolerable in the one next to it or up the hill a ways. As I cleaned up camp and got my bathing suit on, I was sure I was in for a fun time. It turns out that the adjective, fun, didn't even come close to describing the day.

I can hike with the best of them, but a mountain goat I'm not. As I inched forward at a snail's pace, my bent body was rebelling with pain as I climbed higher and higher. There was barely a trail, and I found it hard to imagine that other people came this way often. Wrong! When we finally got to the wild springs my initial thrill of having arrived was instantly replaced with shock at the scene awaiting me. Mother Nature was as breathtaking as Brian had promised, but the people at the pool were a mixture of the ridiculous and the sublime. The ones with their bathing suits on were the good looking ones. The nude ones had bodies like I had never seen before. Fat women with bulging bodies; senior citizens with gray hair that didn't cover nearly enough, and an old hippie, sunning himself on the side of the pool, whose hoary penis looked worn out with age. I was left with the question: Why do the unattractive people display their imperfect bodies, while the bodies worthy of admiration are covered?

* * * * *

The Houston heat didn't bother us at all that summer. Any place we went was air conditioned, and a swim at the apartment pool was the refreshing close to each hot day. I had never before enjoyed idleness more. The lazy days of not having any papers to grade; reading bestsellers, renting classic movies and going to the theatre to see the latest releases; braving the Interstate 45 traffic to spend the late afternoon walking on the Galveston beach, and meeting friends for dinner didn't last nearly long enough. Since there were no teaching jobs for Brian (wood/metal shop and photography), he made arrangements to get on Cypress Fairbanks ISD substitute teachers' list. It was August, thus we needed to drive to Flagstaff before school started mid-month. Divorce papers needed to be signed and he had some more possessions he wanted to move to Houston. As we drove west on Interstate 10, I felt something new and vaguely unsettling, but I didn't name it. Had I, maybe what I was driving toward might not have been such a blow.

The plan was to stay at my friend Kathy Pate's townhouse. That way, I could go with her to The Zoo to get in some dancing while Brian went to see his soon-to-be ex-wife. I certainly didn't have any premonition of disaster as I enjoyed dancing with old friends, and I was not concerned when we got back to Kathy's, and Brian still wasn't home. I was asleep when he came to bed, but I woke up to silence and his body was rigid and still. I didn't say a word, but I felt a distance between us. Not now, I thought sleepily. It will wait until morning. I didn't suspect anything major.

The morning sun was shining brightly into Kathy's beautiful living room. We were alone, and one look at Brian told me that it was major.

"I can't do it, Bonn." were his only words to me.

It took me a minute to believe what he had just said. I couldn't speak and I didn't want to. I got up and walked to the kitchen for more coffee. When I returned, I sat for several minutes in a futile attempt to get my emotions under control. Had I just been kicked in the stomach? I couldn't swallow the coffee so I put the cup down and finally responded.

"So, you are staying? I drive back to Houston alone?" My voice was raspy and I ended with a cough I couldn't contain.

"I'm sorry. Yes, I'm staying. Let me pay my half of the September rent." He placed a check on the coffee table and stood up.

"And your car in Houston?" My voice was almost a whisper.

"I'll fly down next week to get it."

I chose not to say another word. No questions as to why. No begging to reconsider. There was nothing in me that wanted to talk about what had just happened. And, it didn't take me two minutes to gather my clothes and walk to Shotsy. I wondered if I could drive. Probably not a good idea, so I told Brian to go on. I needed to sit in my car until I felt more grounded.

"I am so very, very sorry. Please forgive me." He walked away like he had the weight of the world on his shoulders.

I drove until very late that night. I cried and cried, but I didn't ask why. I just remembered that I had felt a faint stirring of something unwanted as we drove toward Flagstaff yesterday. I guess some part of me knew what was coming. I wasn't mad at Brian, I just felt so empty. And I was so surprised. I had never had this experience before. No one had ever left me. Not even a boyfriend in high school or college. I felt the need to call my daughter, so when I stopped for gasoline I did. She was quick to blame Brian.

"Summer, don't. I feel horrible and I didn't see this coming, but nevertheless, somehow things go the way they do for a reason."

"Oh Mom. I'm so sorry. I don't understand how you can accept things like this the way you do, but I won't say another word against Brian."

"Accept is not the word, Summer. Allow is more like it. The reality is that Brian changed his mind, for whatever reasons. I can't change that happening, no matter how badly I feel about it. So, my only intelligent choice is to not judge it. If I can't practice what I preach, then my beliefs have no real value for my life. Yes, at this moment I can hardly stand it, but I'm going to drive on down this highway back to Houston and go on with life. Thank goodness I have that new teaching job at the Alternative Learning Center. Those criminal types will be a handful. That challenge may prove to be good thing. If I can remember not to judge it as good or bad."

I could hear her sigh before she said, "Mom! I love you. I don't understand you, but I love you. Now, be careful driving and why don't you come to Hallettsville next weekend. We will drink wine and talk about life. I'll let you chose the topics.............as if you don't always."

I was totally drained of all emotion, I thought, as I walked into my empty apartment. How wrong I was. I completely lost it when I opened the door to the kitchen pantry and saw Brian's can of peanuts. I went screaming like a mad woman all the way out to the garbage bin. I had to throw them away. Perfectly good, half-full can of peanuts. As I limped back to the front door, I asked myself, "What good does it do to not pass judgment on some development in your life if you can't control your emotions around it?" Judging from my behavior, we are more emotional creatures than intellectual ones. All my spiritual growth counts for little if my emotional intelligence lags far behind. I locked the door and went on automatic. I guess I would still unpack my suitcase and put everything in its place, even if I was bleeding to death. A cigarette. What I wouldn't give for a cigarette.

I knew Brian would have to contact me because he was coming to get his car. Under the circumstances, I was thinking a brief phone message left while I was at school would be it. Wrong again. I poured myself a glass of wine, sat down on the patio, lit a cigarette, and opened a lengthy letter.

"Dear Bonn,

I feel very strange writing to you. First, I am very, very sorry for the hurt and disappointment I know I have caused you. I'm sure is not easy for you to face your friends and family after you were so happy to tell them about our plans. I am very embarrassed to tell my friends and family what I have done. In fact, so far, I have only told my mother. She was very upset that I had gone back to my wife. Her first comment was, "What about Bonn, don't you love her?" Of course, I had to admit to her that I did. I had a hard time explaining to her, and myself, why I did what I did. I still can't fully explain it to myself. I do know that I felt guilt and sorrow for the pain I was causing my wife. Now I am overwhelmed by those same feelings for what I have done to you. I love my wife like one loves a family member, but not the way one should love a wife. There is no sexual desire or response with her. I seriously wonder if there is something wrong with me. I seem to have let the wrong feelings, and the need for supposed security (sticks and bricks) overtake my need for love and happiness. I am already struggling to fight my negative feelings about Flagstaff, and my doubts about myself. I have that old knot in my stomach, and I have to make a concerted effort not to be depressed. I try to tell myself it is beautiful here, and I go out into the forest to enjoy the beauty, but all I think about is you. I must find a way to stop doing that or I will never be successful at anything here.

Bonn, I really do admire your outlook on life. Don't give up on what you believe. Be true to yourself. You are not weird. Your beliefs did not scare me away. I don't know if I could ever have believed as you do about some of it, but I was very willing to try to understand, and to let you believe as you chose to. The only part that worried me was that you would suddenly decide to give up everything and move away due to some guidance you got via your guides. Remember telling me about how you got the message to move back to Texas after a meditation there in Sedona? Yet, that is exactly what I did to you. The only difference is that I can't point to any guidance in or outside of me. I don't know why I did it, but I imagine you do.

Please believe that I had no preplanned intention to leave you. My wife knows and you should know that the divorce was not cancelled. It was only delayed indefinitely. If I want to reactivate it, I only need to call and ask for a new decree date. Would you believe that I am already thinking about it? Not seriously or often, but the thought does float across my messed up mind. Besides, I have no reason to think that you would take a chance on me again. I can't blame you for that. I have only myself to blame if things don't work out. Please do not think that you are responsible in any way for my decisions and their results. I cannot believe that things were working out so well for you and me, and that I suddenly turned around and walked away from it all. You must think I'm crazy, and maybe I am. I never gave us a chance, and for that I'm afraid I was a fool.

You know that I do love you, and I don't think that will ever stop. You are truly a unique and wonderful woman. I really hope that our relationship continues in some happy way for the rest of our lives. I will get a cab from the airport next Sunday to come for my car. Look for me around 4pm. Let's go to dinner somewhere.

All my love,
Brian"

My good friend Linda Livingston took a very dim view of my decision to spend the night under the same roof with Brian instead of staying over at her house. She was worried that it would be too upsetting for me. And it would have been if I had felt confident that our relationship was over. I didn't, but I probably should have. After all, why would I want a man who leaves his wife, then goes back to her, only to already be questioning that he did? This was certainly new ground for me, and so I wasn't surprised at how inept I was at dealing with it.

My heart fairly jumped at the sight of him. He looked so good. Tall, tanned, easy. I knew the minute I opened the door that I would sleep with him that night and be glad I did. I had decided that I was not going to talk about what had happened. None of the 'why you did me wrong' script of so many movies and books. No! I was going to enjoy our few hours together and make damn sure that he was left with memories of us he would have a hard time forgetting. Somehow it wasn't over. My only concern was, why did I still want him? His track record would not be a recommendation: three divorces it would be, if he got this one. But then, that thought was like the pot calling the kettle black. Just how many times had I been divorced? Three, yes? Yet, I'm fine and he isn't? Really!

I was sure there would be a parting note waiting for me when I got home from work the following day, and there was. I got out of my school clothes, poured myself a glass of wine, and yep, lit a cigarette. The patio was still too hot to enjoy, but I sat down anyway because I never smoked in the apartment. His familiar handwriting brought tears to my eyes. I sat there smoking and sipping the cold wine. I didn't rush to read:

"Dear Bonn,

You have gone to work and I am sitting here alone with my thoughts. My thoughts and I are not good companions right now. I tried to choke down a bowl of cereal and a peach. It took a long time. I reread the note you left me, and I am sorry you think that you are only my current 'fix'. If you were, I wouldn't be sitting here writing this and feeling the terrible emptiness inside. I should be getting on the road, but I just don't feel like it.

There is something very mysterious about us. I had just finished packing and putting everything together in

51

the living room. I was standing there looking at all of it and wondering if I was making the biggest mistake of my life. The possibility of it really hit me hard. I looked up at the phone and thought, 'God, I wish Bonn would call'. Seconds later, you did. I was shocked. I wish I could have been more upbeat for you, but it was a particularly bad moment for me. I was glad that you were sounding better. I was also glad to hear you say that you wanted to be kept up to date on what I'm doing. Somehow, I would also like the same from you. I just don't want to let go of you. I guess that is why I'm still sitting here at 11am, and haven't been to the bank or any place yet.

1:35 PM..........More mystery. You heard my car start this morning, right? So why wouldn't it start this afternoon when I was ready to leave? What's the message? It finally started after about 20 minutes. I went to the bank and closed my checking account. Then I went to Cook Junior High to tell them I wouldn't be available to sub. The new assistant principal, Byron, was very disappointed because they need a long-term sub in my field. The district can't find a certified teacher, therefore, if I got my Texas certification I would get the position. All I would have to do is pass the examination. Now, I really have some things to think about during my drive back to Arizona. Right now I'm feeling much better about me. It's that old job and money and security thing again, I guess. The big question now is, is Bonn an option?

I've got a lot of thinking and decision making to do. I need to think about finding the real Brian. I thought I had found him here in Houston, but he slipped away somehow. Anyway, it will all work out for the best, a very wise person told me. I still don't know what the best will be, but I feel a lot better about it all this afternoon. It's amazing how just the smallest possibility of being with you raises my spirits. I know you won't get overly optimistic about all this because you have concerns of your own.

Well, it's after 2 o'clock and I still have a few things to put in the car. It will be a late drive tonight. Yes, I'll be careful.

Until we meet again somewhere, sometime, somehow, I wish you only the best. Be healthy, be happy, and know that I love you. As the song says, 'I would not have missed it for the world.'

Brian"

CHAPTER FOUR

Fall, Winter, 1996

"Beginnings I Like, and Endings Are Doable...."

Robert Goolrick

Reagh, the father of my children, had been kept up to date by Summer so I wasn't too surprised when he called to ask if he could come for a Saturday night dance and dinner. He had just ended a relationship, and over dinner he voiced weariness with the whole dating game. I was the known to him; there wasn't and wouldn't be an agenda, and he wanted to get out of Dodge occasionally. So, by all means, I could use the company and weekends were designed for dinner out and dancing.

The work week in my new teaching job at Cypress Fairbanks Alternative Learning Center, was the challenge I expected it to be. The challenge I needed to keep my mind off Brian, right? It was that and more. It was a mixed bag. I loved my principal, Terry Rizzo. The small classes made for the best teaching situation, the other teachers were lots of fun and welcoming, and because of the high security on the campus, I was much safer there than in any regular high school in Houston. However, I was afraid of my students and they picked up on that and acted accordingly. During inservice before school began, the science teacher warned me that I would have to watch my back, and that one remark, that I learned later was his idea of a joke, set me up for failure.

I had always been able to establish an easy rapport with my teenage students, but not this time. My classes were small, and predominately boys. I had gang bangers, druggies, misfits, and normal kids caught making a bad choice. Very little difference between these teens and ones I had had last year at Eisenhower High School. And it wasn't a matter of them not behaving appropriately. With my aide, Mr. Smith, a Vietnam vet sitting in the back of the room, no one was tempted to give me trouble. No, that wasn't the problem. It was me. I couldn't feel comfortable with them, and they picked up on my nervousness. My well planned lessons fell flat, and it was my fault, not the boys. The days were turning into weeks, thus I was desperate to change the energy in my classroom. One Friday after school, I didn't dash out as I usually did. Instead, I locked the door, closed the blinds to the afternoon sun, and after turning off the lights, I sat down in one of the student desks to meditate. It took a few minutes to get quiet and relax into my TM. Doing transcendental meditation had been a part of my day since 1988. I had learned to trust the messages I got via the transformation from one level of consciousness to another. And today I had a request to make.

"By virtue of the God Power within me," I began. "I affirm that I am able to understand why I am not relating to my students. I now have the ability to change that, thus enjoy these kids and my day in the classroom." I must have drifted off to sleep following meditation, because I was surprised to wake up. I was sitting there, trying to remember where I was and why, when I realized I was 'thinking'.

'You are reacting to the label placed on your students because they have been sentenced to ALC for some wrongdoing. They are just like all the other students you have had. Some are beyond redemption, others can salvage their lives. These kids need the attention you can give them.

You are famous for caring about your students. You can care about these too. That's why you are here. Remember, there are no accidents. You are in this school on purpose, and you didn't arrange it. The 'powers-that-be' are in charge of your life. Forget about their crimes and devote yourself to getting to know them. Listen to them. That's the best way you can help. They don't have adults in their lives who even make an effort to hear them. And another thing, don't look for positive results from them. Just affirm them as God's children and get on with it. You will be guided and there certainly isn't any one of them that will harm you in any way.'

Wow! What a message. Slowly I got up and out of my now dark classroom. It was way past five o'clock. As I walked through the empty hallway to the front door, the only way in or out of ALC, I felt at home for the first time. I was safe. I was where I belonged, and I was glad to be there. I had turned the corner, yet nothing had changed since sixth period but my perspective. I told Shotsy, as I turned her toward home, "Our thoughts really do create our reality, don't they? These students of mine are not responsible for the fear I have had for them. My thoughts about them did it to me. When am I going to learn to carry that truth with me always? Why do I keep having to be reminded of it? Am I like everyone else? Learning can be accomplished. Changing is another matter, or am I someone who will never be able to 'walk their talk' without constant back-to-basics lessons?" As usual, Shotsy didn't answer me.

Fall in Houston is always so welcomed! The need for air conditioning goes south a bit more each day as October gets older. ALC had become a place I enjoyed being, and I came to expect the weekly letter from Brian. They were newsy: ski trip to Colorado, a drive along the coast of California in a convertible, car races in Arizona, but no matter what or where the activity, he wished I was the one with him. And evidently he was talking to his family about me, because in late September I had gotten a long letter from Margaret Ann, his sister-in-law, whom I had never met.

"Dear Bonn,

.......I'm not one to approve of a third party who breaks up a marriage. This marriage was already broken, and I think your role has been that of friend and confidante. That relationship apparently evolved into something deeper and more special. It must have been quite devastating for you when Brian went back to her. You probably don't want to risk that kind of hurt again. But do you know something odd? The new relationship now happening with your ex-husband sounds very much like Brian's. There's a lot of reference to guilt, weakness, status quo, security, duty, obligation to family, and pleasing someone else. Maybe I've read too much into the 'Bridges of Madison County' version of your relationship with Brian. But I think you both need to give it one more chance.

Brian's being unfair to his wife if he stays with her. If you settle for 'weekends on the ranch', you seem to be unfair to yourself and Reagh. Your children are grown. Having their parents back together sounds like a fairy tale ending, but I've never known it to work any better the second time around.

It's laughable that I am giving unsolicited advice to a woman I've never met. Maybe too many people have told us that multiple marriages spell failure. Maybe not. Maybe they spell growth. Maybe they signal second and third chances at happiness. Brian has, I believe, fallen in love with you. I'm a great romantic. If I were in either person's shoes, I would never retreat to that familiar but boring-yet-safe position. I would throw myself, heart and soul, into an opportunity for sublime happiness. It's worth the risk, I think.

I feel guilty betraying Brian's wife. And, of course, Brian doesn't know I'm writing this. Perhaps I have a selfish motive. From what I know of you, I would like to know you better. You are the genuine article. My brother-in-law has superb qualities. He is vulnerable only because of circumstances. If you two can't get back together, then you really should sever your ties. I'm betting you can't do it. I think you care too much, one for the other.

Life is short. We need someone to dream with - not about. Please excuse my meddling, but I think you belong together.

Love, Margaret Ann"

This letter contributed to my moving closer and closer to deciding to let Brian come back to live with me in Houston. Weekly, he pleaded his case in long letters and phone calls. Actually, our long distance phone visits were more and more about what could be, and less and less about what had happened between us. By mid-November he had reactivated his divorce process and had decided to move to Houston, get certified in Texas so he could then get the teaching job at Dean Middle School, rent an apartment if I didn't want him to live with me, and we would then date and see what developed.

Why didn't I agree to this plan? It certainly was the safest way to proceed. But no. Instead, I decide to let him join me in my two bedroom apartment. I see a pattern here. How many times am I going to get my life just right, only to then risk everything on a major change? I had not forgotten my record since leaving the ranch in the late 1980's.

After my divorce from Reagh, I moved to Houston, got a great teaching job in the Cypress Fairbanks School District, bought a two story, brick home in Spring, TX, redecorated it, almost married Klint. Then I quit my teaching job, sold my home, and moved to Sedona, AZ. It took me months there to get my life under control, but just when I was turning the corner in real estate and had a perfect place to live with roommate Clark, I married Geof. After only one year, I left that marriage and the most beautiful home on the Verde River, to move to Flagstaff where I nearly starved to death, even though I had a great job as Student Teacher Coordinator for Northern Arizona University. Then, almost immediately after I moved back to Sedona to be Clark's housemate once again, I headed back to Texas to find myself living at Cameron's and struggling with teaching government at Eisenhower High School. All of these aspects of my life left much to be desired. So, the gods smiled on me once again: I got the best teaching job of my life at ALC, I had a beautiful apartment with all new furniture, was proud of myself because I lived my days from the spiritual perspective, and I had a social life that included my family in Hallettsville and new friends in Houston, and my parents were close by in Nacogdoches.

I know my history. No one who knows me can claim that I deny reality. I just have this way of acknowledging it, then dismissing it. There is something in me that thrives on change. Wise or not, I'll opt for the major change every time. So naturally I told Brian to join me.

It always feels so good at first. New love is wonderful to live. And the memory of it, years or decades later, can still stir the heart. Ours was a happy life for years, and the fact that our families were included in it contributed to our sense of belonging together. Thanksgiving at the ranch was when my Hallettsville family first met Brian. If there were any bitter feelings floating around Reagh's ranch house, I didn't feel them. Counting the herd of loud children, following my granddaughter Megan's lead, there were over twenty five people in the large, country kitchen or sitting before the fireplace in the living room. I made sure I took lots of photos, because my plan was to send them to Brian's mother, whom I would meet during our Christmas holiday.

Brian looked so good. He wore my favorite of his many colorful sweaters with corduroy pants, and his face still bore remnants of his summer tan. His full head of wavy blond hair was evidence of his youth. He was comfortable talking to everyone, even Reagh. In fact, there was no dynamic of me being the ex-wife. Reagh's current lady friend was in charge, in what was once my kitchen, and there were smiles all around.

All the way back to Houston, we analyzed the day and both of us were very pleased with how well his introduction to my family had gone. "Now, if you just like my family as much as I do yours, life will remain in the perfect position." Brian said,with a wink and a smile, as we hit the Houston traffic.

"Christmas in Ohio! Snow and cold and new people in a new place. It can't miss. You do know, don't you, that I prefer Christmas somewhere other than my house?"

"Not sure I knew that."

"Yep! The several Christmases at LaVoyce's cabin near Creede, CO. started the trend back when my children were very young. Now, after all these years, I make sure that a Christmas trip is how I celebrate the holiday. So, my only worry is that Daddy will be too sick for me to leave him."

"Your parents don't know about me, do they?"

"You know they don't. Nothing against you, of course. It is just that with this cancer thing, this is a stressful time for them. Don't take this personally. It's about me, not you. I am not comfortable with them knowing I have another man in my life. They still think that one day I will go back to the ranch and behave myself."

I still drove to Nacogdoches almost every weekend to see Daddy. I'd try to gauge how the cancer was progressing. Would I get to leave the state and travel all the way to Ohio? I was preparing my parents with the story that I would be spending Christmas with my children, since I had been with them last year. They seemed to be accepting of this, although I felt sure Daddy was hurt that I wouldn't choose to be with him for his last Christmas. Yet he assured me that now because he couldn't even take me to eat catfish on Friday nights, the 25th of December would be just another day. Both my brother in Texas and my sister in Colorado were supportive of our plan to go to Ohio. So it was that the day before we were out of school for the holidays, I decided to risk it.

I had never been east. I thought I preferred the west until I saw the rolling hills of Arkansas, the white fences of the horse farms of Tennessee, the forested mountains of Kentucky, and the Amish homes on their farms in Ohio. Brian was a driving encyclopedia about all the new that I was experiencing. He had been raised in Ohio and had lived with his first wife and two daughters in Pennsylvania for several years. His brother and mother still lived in Bristolville, Ohio, and had for several decades. I especially loved Brian's stories of his mother.

"Mom was born and raised in England," he continued as he drove us on down the highway. "And from all accounts, she was a very beautiful woman and an outstanding dancer."

"I like her already," I said. "Dancing is one of the essentials of life you know," I teased.

"Now that makes me nervous. I can dance, but haven't much."

"Well, it is time you understand that I can't love a man who doesn't dance."

"Right. That makes all the sense in the world." he laughed.

"I don't care. Come New Year's Eve you will realize how serious I am about dancing. But never mind now. I want to know more about your mom."

"I remember her as always having cooked enough for dinner so my friend Henry could eat at our house without any previous arrangement. If she was unhappy, I never knew it because she didn't complain. Every Saturday night she and Dad went dancing. I sort of knew that he could have lived just fine without it, but he did it for her. She worked hard, yet I sensed that she thought of herself as the queen. She never learned to drive, but that didn't keep her home. It was either my father's duty or mine or my brother's to take her where she wanted to go. And where she wanted to go was shopping. Many's the time I have sat in the car or walked up and down the sidewalk in front of the department store waiting for her. You'll see. She had, and still does have, the most jewelry and clothes of anyone I have ever known"

"Does she stay dressed up all the time?"

"Well, pretty much so. If she is around the house, she has a housecoat for every day of the week, but if she goes out anywhere, she dresses to the nines. Even if it is an emergency. I'll never forget the time she slammed a sliding glass door on her finger and I had to rush her to the emergency room. The doctor was a cute guy and she was having fun flirting with him until she realized that she didn't have her earrings on. My God, she had a major meltdown right then and there."

Brian laughed, but then his story went in a different direction. "Don't get me wrong. Mom isn't just a fluff. She worked herself almost to death taking care of Dad before we had to put him in a nursing home. Due to Alzheimer's, he had to be watched almost constantly, and too, he started getting violent. That was too much for her to handle physically. Even so, she would have preferred him to be laying on the couch where she could see him - not in the nursing home."

"Has she been able to get on with her life now that he is dead? Does she go out socially?" I was hoping she had the pleasure of a whole new life after those years of tending a sick husband.

"Yes she does, but I'm not sure she enjoys it all that much. She complains that the Senior Center is full of old people. Clearly, she doesn't see herself as one, even though she is in her late eighties. But going there every week does give her a reason to dress up. Hope you will want to go with me while we are there. She is fun to watch. I've never seen a woman, any age, that can work a room the way she can. All the men just love her."

The plan was to go by Brian's brother's home first, so we did. What a welcome we got. Two fat, friendly dogs barked and barked. John and Margaret Ann were cheerful and warm. Their home smelled like Christmas, and I relaxed into what felt like my family. Then, after a short visit for making plans for the next couple of days, we drove on to Hilda's. She met us at the door. Her high, resounding voice rang out to us, and her eyes were shining with glee. What a beautiful woman, I thought, as I shook her hand and stepped into her warm house out of the frigid cold early evening.

"Oh Brian. Brian." Hilda just melted into his arms.

"Hi Mom! As gorgeous as ever. Got anything to eat?"

"Oh you. Come on in this house. Of course I have dinner ready. My pot roast has been on since this morning."

"Do we have time for one cocktail before we eat? Bonn loves to have a scotch, and if I remember correctly, you like scotch."

I thought she was going to cry. I have never seen anyone so thrilled over the prospect of a drink. Brian had told me that his brother didn't approve of her drinking wine or liquor. Seems there had been concern years earlier that Hilda and Bernard drank a bit much. With all the dinner parties; the vacation weeks in Florida, and the every Saturday night dancing, drinking was a part of their social life.

"Oh my yes. I just love scotch, but I don't have any soda in the house. Is water okay, Bonn?"

That broke the ice. The evening went perfectly. The roast was good, but I have never eaten an apple pie like Hilda's. She was full of chatter and fun, and her parting comment of the evening left us rolling on the bed and trying to muffle our laughter.

We were following her down the hall when she said, "Here is your bedroom. Brian, you remember that it has the queen size mattress. I presume you sleep together."

The next two days of our visit went so well. Margaret Ann's Christmas dinner was spectacular. The gift opening took forever, but I liked the idea of it being a 'one-at-a-time' arrangement. Hilda and I entertained by dancing together. I was always a good leader, so we did a 50's jitterbug to wild applause. Our evenings in Hilda's home were the perfect end to full days. I took my place on the couch, Brian in his dad's chair, and Hilda in her own recliner. We made plans. She would come to visit us next summer. When school was out, we would come for her. We would travel through the south first before heading back to hot Houston. She was thrilled to learn that Galveston was only an hour's drive from where we lived. Much too soon, it was time to head back to Texas. She stood in the door and waved us goodbye with tears in her eyes. We felt bad knowing how much she wanted to leave with us that minute.

The last day of the year was celebrated in my favorite way. Brian and I had made it back in time to plan to go out to dinner and dancing with my friend Linda and her new guy. Daddy was holding his own; I went to see him the minute we got back to Houston, and I was still glowing from the memories of the wonderful Ohio Christmas trip. For New Year's Eve, I chose a short, black sweater dress with lots of gold bling, and black lace hose and very high heels to wear. Brian was handsome in his dark suit and tie. All was festive until we walked into Linda's house.

If only her date hadn't been such a jerk. Was it possible that a grown man could have a meltdown over the way his vest fit him? We were there for a drink before going on to dinner, and it didn't take me two minutes to decide he was a loser. I was tempted to find fault with Linda for her not showing him the door. I am always quick to judge women who allow men to mistreat them. I understand that this doesn't serve me well, and if I can't yet keep from doing it, at least I realize I shouldn't do it. Maybe one day I'll graduate, but not tonight.

The food was really good, and the dance music was slow and romantic. That is probably why I didn't notice that Brian really wasn't a good dancer. We had a wonderful time. Lots of pretty people in a crowded room, and we rang in the new year with champagne and a long, passionate kiss. We were as happy as Linda was miserable.

1997! It was the best beginning of a new year since my return to Texas. Everything was in place for full time happiness. Brian was subbing at Dean Middle School in the vocational department. He was studying to take the Texas certification test so he could be hired as the teacher. My life at the ALC was wonderful. I was teaching American history and this subject gave me lots of wiggle room for fun projects. When we were studying the Roaring 20's, I turned the classroom into a Speak Easy, and taught the boys how to Charleston. A boy from South America turned out to be the star. This young man had not spoken one word to anyone since coming to ALC. He wasn't hostile, just missing-in-action.

Every student had to participate. They had to attempt the several Charleston steps I was teaching them. What a hilarious sight. Those tough criminal-types lined up to attempt to twist on the balls of their feet. Terry, my principal, and some of the other teachers joined us. Then, I noticed my silent student, and I was amazed. He was good! Without any obvious effort, he could easily do any step I demonstrated.

So, I started dancing with him alone. I did steps he could follow, and all of a sudden the whole class was cheering him on. The bell rang, and class was over. He was beaming with pride as he left the room. "See you Miss," were the first words I had ever heard him say.

I was keeping a 'Gratitude Journal'. It was a suggestion from the Simple Abundance Class I was taking at my neighborhood church. Every night I would make an entry, and it never took me two minutes to jot down all my blessings:

January 14, 1997

1. Electricity - after much of yesterday spent without, I now am reminded of how all of life depends on it.

2. Brian - a 'nothing special' day, but that makes no difference. I just love looking across the breakfast table at him or previewing a World War II movie for my classes with him. He is the biggest blessing in my life.

3. My job at ALC - I'm fighting the Sunday night blues on Tuesday because we had two days off because of ice and snow. Yet I do love this teaching criminals. The classes are small and I have a boy named Colby in world history that motivates me to go the extra mile. He stopped by after school last week to ask about how to meditate. He is a graduating senior who has lost his scholarship in drama because of a drinking episode on a school trip. Depression has set in for the first time in his young life, and I am trying to help him every way I can. I understand his parents have just about disowned him.

4. Our dreams and plans - It can feel good and scary at the same time. Brian and I starting out at the ages of 58 and 59. We are insane, but we don't tell each

other. We have a realtor looking for us a house to buy.

5. Daddy seems to be getting closer to his next adventure. I'm so glad. My sister LaVoyce said tonight that he sleeps all the time. Thank God she could come to stay with Mom and Dad during these last days of his life.

6. My life with Brian - I just love living with him. Everything is happier: eating dinner; going for a walk, watching a movie, seeing him at the desk paying bills.

7. For the possibility of Hampton Roads Publishing Co. accepting my book, *Higher Ground, One Woman's Journey.* I plan to hand deliver it when we drive up the east coast during spring break. I am almost finished with the corrections my editor wants made.

Daddy died on Mother's birthday in January. I got the call at school. It was a relief to know that his suffering was over. Brian and I stayed in the home of my friend Carol Willis in Nacogdoches. Since Mother didn't know anything about Brian, we had to be careful. He attended the funeral, but he didn't sit with me and Mother didn't notice him.

The large parlor in the funeral home was packed. All of Daddy's many friends were there, and his relatives came from all over the state to pay homage. Having attended so many funerals in the past few years, he knew exactly what he wanted, therefore he had planned it all. The men in his Sunday school class were the honorary pallbearers, but his six grandsons did the actual honors. The sermon was short, the songs were the traditional Baptist ones, and I managed to give a short talk I felt sure he loved. However, the surprise of the day was learning that Daddy's plan included treating all of his children, grandchildren and great grandchildren to a meal together at 'the catfish place' following his burial. We knew he was there with us. Daddy, Uncle Ford, Ford, and Granddaddy had lived a full life, and we were happy to celebrate it.

The spring months flew by, all loaded with blessings. I loved having my granddaughters, Megan and Cody, come for weekend visits. Since the pool was closed, we spent more time and more of my money at the mall. Both of the sunshine girls could go from country to city without blinking. They got that ability from me, and Brian was fast becoming a favorite with them, and of course, that pleased me too.

We went east again during spring break, but this time we didn't go to Ohio. We went to New Jersey and Washington DC to see his two daughters. And yes, I was a little nervous. It was probably too much to hope for the kind of reception I had gotten in Ohio last Christmas.

Cathy, Brian's oldest, lived in a high rise apartment she owned in Chevy Chase, Maryland.

"Man, what a world," I said. "I could do this." People everywhere, and city lights on bright.

"You do, Silly. You live in Houston, TX" Brian reminded me.

"We live miles from downtown, and this feels like downtown to me. Do you see any pine trees like we have around our patio?"

Cathy was a beautiful version of her dad. Very tall, blond, statuesque, and calm. Cereal for breakfast too. She was welcoming, but I learned later that Brian had not given her much notice of our visit. A habit that showed itself more than once during this trip. For a detail oriented guy, this didn't fit.

Chris and her husband Steve, were newly transplanted from sunny California. Both were struggling a bit with the New Jersey cold, wet, snowy scene. Chris took the metro into Manhattan every work day, and Steve was in the process of reinventing himself. Their two story home on a tree lined street was typical suburbia and would be perfect for the family they were planning to have. Our ride into New York on the metro was a treat for me. Central Park and coffee at the Plaza Hotel made my day.

As we drove towards Maryland to see one of Brian's best friends, an artist bachelor, I got him to talk about his girls.

"I wasn't around them much when they were growing up, and I regret that now. I moved across the country to California, and this left their mom to see them through their teenage years. She did a wonderful job, so she is the one to get the credit for how they turned out."

"I guess you were really pleased when Chris decided to attend college in California."

"You bet I was. Thanks to that, I got to spend more time with her than I ever did with Cathy. Maybe that will even out one of these days. You know how Cathy never writes my address in ink. My children, like yours, know me to be a rolling stone."

The weeks were headed for summertime, and I needed to tell Mother about Brian! She was now living in College Station where my brother was tending to her, and so one spring Sunday we drove over for an introduction. Nothing heavy like 'this is the man I sleep with', just a casual 'This is Brian. We met in Flagstaff, and he now lives in Houston too.'

If she was interested, it didn't show. This was typical behavior for her, and for the first time I welcomed it. With Morgan, my sister-in-law, in the mix, there was nothing but casual, light conversation. The fact that Morgan was everyone's favorite was well deserved. Her very presence in a room lifted the energy, and she certainly worked her magic for me that day. I was relieved that Mother was now in the loop. The fact that I hadn't told her we were living together didn't concern me. She might never know, and that would be fine.

The minute school was out we were on the road. We had our differences, but our love for travel was not one of them. I could sit in a car as long as he could. And, I had developed a way to keep him happy while driving, and me free to think my own thoughts. Brian was a walking encyclopedia about cars. Classic and current. All I had to do was ask a question about the history of some model, and he was good for miles. Evidence of my long held notion that men need an audience more than any other thing.

Brian's mother Hilda was a joy to be around. During the long road trip from Ohio, she entertained me with her stories. She was never tired or grumpy or displeased. Everything was wonderful. I had never been around anyone who was so thrilled with every day. Such a contrast from my mother. Maybe that was why I was so impressed. I truly enjoyed her company, and it was in Mississippi when we were staying in a plantation home, turned bed and breakfast, that I called her Scarlet for the first time. She had finally climbed up into the feather bed and was sighing over the comfort and glamour of it when I entered her room to say goodnight.

"Why my lands, Miss Scarlet, you are as pretty as a picture laying there in that fine bed." I said with a southern accent and a bow. "Now Honey, is there any little ole thing I can get you before you retire for the evening?"

She loved it. Hilda clapped her hands and just laughed and laughed. It fit her perfectly. Scarlet, not Hilda. From then on, I called her Scarlet more often than I did Hilda.

After spending three weeks with his mother, I had a better understanding of Brian. Naturally, we are all products of our DNA and environment. I now got that her love for shopping was the reason for his dislike of it. He thought I was an angel for taking her, day after day, to buy more clothes. She liked to bargain shop, so this meant going from place to place, never mind Houston traffic. To tell the truth, it did get to me. Personally, I only went shopping when I had a definite need. Never was it entertainment, as it was for Hilda. However, because it thrilled her so, and I knew that she didn't get to do this in Ohio, I rose to the occasion. It helped too, that Brian would take over the minute we hit the apartment. He would make her a cocktail; I would go to the kitchen to make dinner, and they would sit on the patio while she re-lived her day for him.

We certainly did go out of our way to entertain her, and she appreciated it so much. The day we drove almost to Dallas to take her to a rodeo was the limit. First of all, the fact that she could wear a western dress of mine and boots too, was the icing on her cake. She posed for photos in my cowgirl outfit, and you could tell that she was so pleased with herself. She thrived on attention, and her behavior at the rodeo got it for her.

"Wheeeeeee! Go, go, go!" Her voice rang out loud and clear. "Ride em, cowboy! Hang on!"

I looked over at Brian and his face was blood red. He was embarrassed, that was obvious.

"Oh Honey, she is just enjoying herself," I whispered. I didn't mind at all that people were turning to look in our direction.

"This is just what she used to do at my basketball games," he hissed. Hilda must have heard him.

"Oh, am I being too loud? I'm sorry, Brian." Hilda was instantly hushed. "Bonn, did you know that I had to stop going to his games because of my cheering. I just get so excited that I forget myself."

During the drive back to Houston I learned something else about Brian, via his mom.

"Bonn, this is just the greatest western dress I have ever worn. Thank you so much for letting me wear it."

"Yeah Mom, what you wear is really important to you, isn't it?"

This was the nearest thing to a criticism that I had heard Brian say to his mother, and she was hurt.

"I know I did the wrong thing when you were in first grade Brian. But are you ever going to forgive me?"

"It's okay Mom. Really." was all he could manage.

"Well, I am going to tell Bonn what happened. If he had been a girl it would have been fine, but being a boy, it wasn't. I would dress him all up with suspenders, knee britches, and a string tie like the children wore in England. Of course, that just got him teased by the other kids. It wasn't until he developed asthma, and the doctor told me to change the way I dressed him, that I realized what I had done. To this day, I am very sorry."

Only a few days after we put Hilda on the plane to Ohio, we headed north to Colorado. It felt good to be alone again. We were driving to Creede, CO, my favorite place on earth. My sister's cabin was about 20 miles out of town in a development called Ptarmigan Meadows. I had been going there for Christmases and 4th-of-July-weeks for years. I knew Brian was going to love it. We could hike all day, and sit in front of the fireplace at night to rest our weary bones. No television corrupted the room, and after a week's meals, I was always a size larger.

"How long has it been since you fixed fence, Brian?" My brother-in-law Tom, was the breakfast chef. LaVoyce didn't do mornings, so you never saw her in the kitchen during the am.

"Could be never, but I'm handy with tools. Probably could give you some help." Brian was staring at Tom again. If Hilda's preoccupation with clothes bothered him, Tom's total disregard for his appearance got his attention as well. As long as I could remember, Tom had made breakfast in the same bright gold, grease stained satin housecoat.

"Good, good. There is a committee gathering this morning to walk the fences. After every winter, we mend fence. Love to have you join us."

Hours later, LaVoyce and I were sitting on the front porch, and we could hear the voices of the men walking the property. Sure enough, Brian was leading the pack. He probably was a few years younger than most of them, but his edge was his good physical condition. That night, my sister added to his role as free-laborer.

"Brian," she asked in her most charming way. "You aren't claustrophobic are you?"

He straightened up on the couch and asked why. Cautious man that he is.

"Well, we really need to clean out the ash box under the cabin, and the boys usually do it for us. Tom has a hard time getting under the house because of his belly. No offense, Dear (his term of endearment for her)".

"None taken, you can be sure My Dear. If you can get Brian under the house instead of me, you can say what you want about my body." He was smiling and his eyes were twinkling. Tom was not a handsome man, but there was something sensual about him. His wit and teasing way got him way down the road. I had always enjoyed his company, although I knew he did not care for me. It wasn't anything personal. LaVoyce had explained him to me years ago. He just didn't have a very high regard for women. Courtesy of his mother, of course.

The entire day of the 4th was celebration from beginning to end. Tom cooked fried trout, potatoes and onions and biscuits for breakfast. This was to last us, with only junk food in town, until the big feed at Freemon's Ranch that evening. After we found a parking place and were walking down the one main street in Creede, I recognized the sheriff, the bartender at the Old Miners Inn, the Mountain Man rafter, and a few of the summer folks at the parade in town. It was such fun and the weather was perfect. After going in every jewelry shop in town (my favorite is Rare Things), and watching several mining contests in mid-afternoon, we drove back to the cabin for a rest and change of duds. The evening started early with drinks at the bonfire at Freemon's, followed by a feast of barbeque with all the trimmings. It was close to dark when we drove into town to see the fireworks and then go dancing.

"You don't mind if I dance, do you?" I knew Brian could be trusted to tell me the truth.

"Of course not. That gets me off the hook. Besides, I enjoy watching much more than dancing myself."

There were plenty of guys to dance with, so I was fine with the evening. Still, it was a disappointment that we didn't have the love of dancing in common. It would be years later before I held this against him. My needing the man in my life to be all things to me, eventually proved to be fatal to our relationship. There was a psychic in Houston who had warned me years ago that I gave men too many jobs. She had insisted that I needed to decide what was most important to me: money, looks, sex, or intellect. Settle for one or two, and be grateful. I could hear the truth in what she said, but I was never able to follow her advice.

Initially, Brian being hired as a teacher in the Cypress Fairbanks School District made him a new man. He didn't get the news until late July and school begins mid-August. It was a brand new vocational department at Cook Junior High and he was in charge of getting it all organized and ready for the students. It all sounded wonderful until he saw how unfinished the interior of the building was. The other teacher hired was just a kid right out of college. He was going to have his work cut out for him, but neither one of us realized how hard it was going to be on him. Everything about the job went against Brian's natural bent. I could not have done it. I would not have done it. He did. But he paid a high price.

My teaching job, on the other hand, was getting better with every year that passed. My principal, Terry, was the best boss I had ever had. No games or power struggle between us. She appreciated the effort and interest I took in my lessons and the students, and I was grateful for the way she trusted my judgment to do the right thing in the classroom. And, we always got a laugh out of the way the kids referred to her as 'the other gray headed lady'. In fact, now that I was teaching American history to sophomores, I created units of study following World War II beginning with the 1950's. When we were delving into the culture of the 50's, I had Terry join me in a demonstration of the jitterbug. Naturally, I led and she was a great partner. As the day progressed and rumors flew around the small school about what was going on in my classroom, other teachers and administrators joined my students to watch us 'gray headed ladies' dance. The room full of cheering folks motivated us to really 'put on the dog'. Terry could still twirl on a dime, and my footwork was 'college days' good.

Now that Brian had a full time teaching job, our shopping for a house during the weekends got more serious. Naturally Brian wanted to be as far out of town as possible, so we shopped at first in the forested areas around the small town of Magnolia. However, when we would clock the time it took us to drive to our jobs, we discarded that hope. Then one Sunday we found just what we were looking for in northwest Houston, about midway between our schools.

Brian was happiest about the house having a three car garage. He had plans to spend his spare time restoring a classic car. In the meantime, he was having fun attending Saturday night car shows and entering and winning trophies with his Mustang convertible he had purchased from his daughter Cathy.

The house was the usual three bedroom, two bath, brick, one story subdivision house. Nothing dramatic or special, but it was new and affordable. I was excited to at last have a bedroom to use as an office. I could now spend many hours putting finishing touches to my first book in total privacy. Too, there was a community pool just up the street, and my granddaughter Cody loved it. She would jump into the middle of the neighborhood kids and announce, 'Let's play'. It was while her dad and I were watching her swim one hot Saturday afternoon that he told me that he had decided to get a divorce. I welcomed this news at the time. Years later, however, when her mother would take her to California, it felt like a very high price to pay for my son's happier life.

Summertime again, and not a minute too soon. Brian was exhausted. Dealing with junior high students without a completed vocational facility had been rough. Thank God no one got hurt, but there were some close calls. Yes, a thirteen year old will try out his electric drill on a classmate's eye goggles. Like me, Brian thought of the summer months as travel time. This year we would be going east again, camping our way to Ohio. Surprisingly, I was in a better mood about it than Brian.

I didn't realize until we were weeks into finding the perfect spot for our tent; cooking on the camp stove; walking in the dark with a flashlight to the bathroom, and visiting with the other campers in their RV's that Brian was getting more and more depressed about our modest tent living. When he was married before, they had a fancy camper with all the bells and whistles. He didn't sleep on the ground, or wake up to dew on everything. Lucky for me, I didn't have his frame of reference. Sure, I got tired of the meal preparation challenge, but I wasn't feeling mistreated. Nevertheless, I was glad to get to Hilda's. A roof over my head and a kitchen had never looked so good to me. Not to mention, a bathroom right down the hall. I could lay on the extra long couch and read all day while Brian did the 'honey do's' for his mom. Too, the car shows were the most spectacular I had ever attended. Brian explained to me that the guys spent the long, cold Ohio winters in their garages perfecting their cars to be shown and win awards during the short summers. Eventually, I got my fill of classic cars, so I would stay home with 'Scarlet' and let Brian and his brother enjoy the shows together. Both of them were car enthusiasts. However, that was almost the only thing they had in common. His brother had lived his life in the same town, in the same house, with the same wife, working at the same job; thinking the same thoughts and running the same errands. Brian had lived in many states, had had several jobs in building construction and education, had three very different wives, and had traveled the world. But on a Saturday night at a car show in Ohio, anyone would think that they had never spent a day apart in their lives.

Brian's lifelong friend, Henry, was my kind of guy. He and his wife, Donna, knew how to throw the best dinner parties I have ever attended. They had lived in the same apartment on the Kent State Campus forever. Henry had been an English professor there and Donna too worked at the university. When Henry lost the use of his strong voice for the classroom, he then turned to his hobby of painting to fill his days and pockets. I loved his art and it was displayed in every room of their tiny two story apartment.

"Come in, Bonn. I love meeting all of Brian's women." The twinkle in his eyes and the tinkle of his glass predicted a fun evening.

"And, my dear man, I understand that it was Hilda's cooking that pulled you through puberty."

"And that's for sure," he said as he gave me a hug. "That woman could cook. Come in and meet the one I live with now."

Donna joined us from the kitchen. She was a tiny, darling woman with eyes that could penetrate your soul. "Yes, I was Henry's first choice and he hasn't had the energy to replace me. What can I fix you to drink?"

With that the evening was off and running. The other three dinner guests were well educated and well traveled people, thus the conversation was varied and lively. Food and drink was abundant, and so was the good cheer. It was almost eleven when I stumbled to the car for the hour drive back to Hilda's. I was glad that Brian never drank too much. Unlike me. Not often, but tonight anyway. I did better at his high school reunion.

It was a full day of visiting the school, having lunch at the burger joint on the lake, and dancing with Henry after a grand dinner that night. All Brian's classmates were interested in his latest life. Many had remained in Ashtabula, the town on Lake Erie where he had been raised. Actually, he and Henry had lived the largest lives and were the most colorful of all the classmates. Brian's girl friend had married a local guy and had raised their Catholic children there. His old vocational building was still in use and Brian loved passing his hands over the tools he had used. And of course, he and the other basketball stars had to attempt a few baskets in the gym. Brian's picture was in the Hall of Fame. I learned that he had been an outstanding basketball player. Mercy, he was thin! His coach had him on an eating regime that didn't look like it put one pound on him. Two lunches in the cafeteria; a full meal after school made by his girlfriend's Italian mother, and then another dinner later that night at home.

Summers never last long enough. Especially now that public schools begin their fall semester in mid August. Brian was noticeably more quiet during the two day drive back to Texas from the east. He now knew what was ahead of him at Cook Junior High. Sure, the vocational lab was more complete than last year, but the kind of students channeled into his program were not ones he would ever elect to have. Too many of them were kids who didn't have any interest in learning anything, much less how to construct projects. But what made it so nerveracking for Brian was that it was a dangerous course to put them into. Teenagers don't really have a sense of mortality anyway, so to spend time going over the safety rules didn't guarantee that anyone would be safer. Too, Brian was a law and order man, and discipline of any kind was not part of the junior high public school experience. How many times have I said that I would take in ironing before I taught that age group. Then one afternoon, a few weeks after school started, I got to see first hand what

Brian's work world was like. They were in the classroom and full of questions for me.

"Does Mr. B let you drive his Mustang?" The black convertible parked outside the door of the vocational building was Brian's only claim to fame. Most of the kids thought he was a hard ass, but one and all just loved his car.

"He would, if I could." I answered with a wink at him. "You see, it takes someone who really knows cars to work the gears. I'm just not good with anything other than an automatic. So no, not really. The last time I tried driving it my granddaughter, Cody, was with me. I couldn't get it into second gear, and I said 'shit'. She really scolded me and said that I needed to write that word one hundred times."

The fact that I would say 'shit' really endeared me to them. I knew it would. After all, I taught the high school bad guys, thus I knew what turns them on. Several hands were waving for my attention.

"Do you make more money than Mr. B?" asked a pretty little girl without one bit of awareness that this question was inappropriate.

I turned to Brian and said, "I do, don't I?"

"I don't really know. You keep the books, so you tell me." Brian was having as much fun as his students.

"Tell me first, why do you ask?"

The immediate response was, "Because you dress lots better than he does."

"Thank you, and you're right. I sure do." I said with a laugh, but Brian's was louder. "I have time for one last question. Who will it be? Okay, young man. Lay it on me."

"Why are you so white and Mr. B is so red?"

The only thing I could do is say something ridiculous: "Because I am so old and he is so young."

I could still hear them clapping and yelling as I opened the door and headed down the hall. I had a feeling that the mood in Brian's classroom was not the usual one. Such a shame for all involved.

There was another cloud over our life now. Not only Brian's very difficult teaching assignment, but the results of his annual required physical added a new subject matter for our days. Now mind you, Brian didn't even have a doctor. He couldn't remember ever having one. He was the picture of health, never sick, didn't smoke and never had, drank very little, was slim and exercised religiously. Nevertheless, tests showed that he had an irregular heart beat that needed treatment. Meaning medication. Thus began the chapter in Brian's life entitled, 'How Can This Be?' I guess it is a good thing we don't know the future. Eleven years to live isn't a very long time, when you are only fifty eight.

Life for me, minus Brian's challenges, was only getting better. My teaching assignment had been changed to a new program that Cypress Fairbanks ISD had purchased called 'Teen Leadership'. And it had been my principal, Terry, who knew I would be perfect as the facilitator. I was thrilled to know that at last I was going to get to use some of my personal interests in the classroom. Sure teaching history is fine, but these kids needed to be students of themselves more than anything else. My first love had always been psychology anyway, and the fact that I was now going to get to help students develop their emotional intelligence and a sense of personal responsibility for their lives, had me walking on cloud nine. During the August teacher inservice days, Terry and I put our heads together to design a new learning experience for ALC students. I was positive that this course was going to be 'just what the doctor ordered' for these kids who were already, officially, struggling with life.

"Okay, but tell me why you want to turn your classroom into a living room/dining room scene", Terry said to me as she was walking into my classroom, while hanging up her cell phone (she never did just one thing at a time).

I wasn't sure I had her attention, but I jumped right in. "This is not an academic course so we can do without the student desks. But moreover, I want the kids to get that the time spent with me in this social environment is about them. They have much to learn, but I want it to be a more casual energy in this room. I'm hoping to get away from 'I'm the teacher who knows everything, and 'you are the student who must learn it for a grade' atmosphere."

I wasn't totally convinced that Terry would actually let me do everything I wanted to do. She was the best principal I had ever had, and she had always supported all my projects, but I wasn't outside the box teaching English or history. This course, that all the students would be required to take, was right off the press. Too, after attending the workshop for all the district's Teen Leadership teachers, I knew how I could incorporate some of my ideas around how to teach teenagers to live more consciously. I wouldn't be teaching just from the prepared text. No, I would use the basics of TL, but I certainly would not be limited to the author's printed page.

Terry sat looking at me for what seemed like a long time. Her sandaled foot was kicking up and down at a fast clip. She leaned forward over her shapely, crossed leg and in her brisk, 'this is the way it is going to be' tone finally said, "What do you have in mind? You know, of course, that there is no money for furniture. It was all I could do to get this new program for our school. You are an expensive teacher, and to pull you out of academics and have you devote the entire day to TL took some tall talking. I operate on the theory that I will get my way because of my long tenure with the district, and all these gray hairs; nevertheless, I watch how far I stick my neck out." Terry laughed her throaty, cigarette-affected chuckle.

"Terry, you don't have to worry about furniture. I have a dining room set, a couch, lamps and end tables I can contribute. I'll pick up a few floor pillows and they won't cost me much."

"You do realize, don't you, that you can't depend on your furniture not getting much worse for the wear. Remember, many of these kids don't even have homes. They might not be as respectful of your things as you would think."

"It's okay. I don't expect to keep any of it. Brian and I are talking about moving out west after I retire, and I have no desire to haul furniture across country. So, don't worry about that."

Terry stood up and headed for the door. She opened it and turned to me and said, "All right then. Just make sure you have your detailed lesson plans into me every Friday for the following week. I want to know what you are doing, and it is not because I don't trust you. It's just that this is a new program for the district and no one, other than me, thought ALC should get it too. I don't want any surprises."

I smiled to myself when Terry closed the door. She was the kind of principal I had never had before coming to ALC. I really respected how she ran a tight ship, how she was so decisive, how she took pleasure in her job, (that for her, could last into the evenings), and how she kept a sharp, protective eye on all her teachers. Years ago she had almost been killed in an automobile accident, but she survived to continue her career in Cy Fair. She was the one chosen by the district to open and operate an alternative school for kids in trouble. Yes, Terry was a force within the Texas educational circle, and I knew how blessed I was to have her as my boss. There would be no way I would jeopardize the confidence she had in me. I moved the student desks into the hall. I plotted where the couch and dining table would fit best, then I turned on some mood music to play while I designed my first week's lesson plans.

From the first day of school, my routine with my students began at the door each day. I would shake their hand and greet them by name. This was the best time to gauge their mood. It is a better plan to know they are having a bad day than to have to deal with it after they have demonstrated such during class. And, no student ever took advantage of me telling them to let me know, as they were coming into class, that they were stressed.

When the tardy bell rang the door was locked, and designated students for that week would turn off the overhead lights and start the Arizona Indian flute music. As the days passed and they became comfortable with this routine, I could almost hear their collective sigh as they got comfortable and shut their eyes. Due to the nature of ALC, there would be new students joining my class all during the school year. None of them were thrilled to be sentenced to ALC, thus you can imagine their attitude when faced with a classroom situation that was totally unfamiliar to them. Quite without my instigating it, a member of the class would react to the new student's behavior. When he had had enough of the new kid's protests, he would say something like this: "Shut up Fool. Just close your eyes and be alone with yourself."

I would be hard pressed to say which I enjoyed more, the designing of the lessons or living them. No class ever responded alike. Many times I was totally surprised with some reaction of a student. Always, I loved every minute of it. And, my students learned that the course was really and truly about them. I told them that they would get out of it what they put into it, and most all of them took every lesson seriously. Sure, once in a while a student would not cooperate, and they would be led from the classroom by my assistant. They would lose their points for that class period, and since they were working their way out of ALC, that was punishment enough.

I decided to begin the course with a lesson based on Cherie Carter-Scott's book, *If Life Is A Game, These Are The Rules*. The author makes the statement that "There are no mistakes in life, only lessons that are repeated." In light of them being sentenced to ALC for some wrong doing, I was sure that would get their attention.

LESSON OBJECTIVE: To consider our common human condition in relation to our primary spiritual nature.

INTRODUCTORY SCRIPT: "Life has often been compared to a game. We are never told the rules, unfortunately, nor given any instructions about how to play. We simply begin at birth and make our way through the years, hoping we play it right. Many of us don't even exactly know the objective of living, nor what it means to actually win. That is what 'The Rules For Being Human' is all about. These are the guidelines to playing the game we call life. However, they are not magic. They are just a sort of road map for you as you travel your path to more self awareness." Cherie Carter-Scott

The Rules For Being Human
by Cherie Carter-Scott

1. You will receive a body. You may like it or hate it, but it will be yours for your entire lifetime. (The body is the major part of your humanness; consider the time, money, interest, emotion you have around your body.)
2. You will learn lessons. You are enrolled in a full-time school called life.
3. Each day in this school you will have the opportunity to learn lessons. You may like the lessons or think them irrelevant and stupid.
4. There are no mistakes, only lessons. Growth is a process of trial and error; experimentation. The 'failed' experiments are as much a part of the process as the experiment that ultimately 'works'.
5. A lesson is repeated until learned. A lesson will be presented to you in various forms until you have learned

it. When you have learned it, you can then go on to the next lesson.

6. Learning lessons does not end. There is no part of life that does not contain its lessons. If you are alive, there are lessons to be learned.

INSTRUCTIONS: Read as one, questions 2,3,4,5,6. Consider/discuss together. Possible topics for class consideration to interject: How do you feel about the word 'lesson'? Does it put a bad taste in your mouth? Do you like the idea that 'life' is one big lesson that is never over? Can you accept the idea that there is no such thing as a mistake? Why/why not? Have you noticed any patterns in your life or the lives of others? Would these patterns be evidence that until one 'gets it', the situation keeps coming around, again and again? Ask for examples from their experiences. Share from your life.

7. 'There' is no better than 'here'. When your 'there' has become a 'here', you will simply obtain another 'there' that will again tend to look better than 'here'. This is called living in the future. A 'something' in the future will make you happier? What is the danger in living your life like that? Why do so many people live in the future rather than in the present? Consider the concept that, 'You take yourself wherever you go."

8. Others are merely mirrors for you. You cannot love or hate something about another person unless it reflects to you something you love or hate about yourself. Examples: You dislike someone because they can't keep a secret. Ask yourself if you keep secrets? You hate the way your boyfriend/girlfriend criticizes you so much. Notice if you have the habit of criticizing your parents, teachers, friends, yourself.

9. What you make of your life is up to you. The CHOICE is yours. Discuss: Yes, but what if I'm a minority, my parents are poor/divorced/unloving, I am handicapped, or I'm not a good student?

10. Your answers lie inside you. The answers to all of life's questions lie INSIDE YOU. All you need to do is look, listen, trust, and sometimes wait. (So how does one communicate with the 'whatever' in each of us that has our answers? Meditation and dreams have been experienced as the means for this inner communication).

11. You will most likely forget all of this and probably return to your tendency to say, "Why is this happening to me?" (The victim mentality is very popular in our culture. Taking full responsibility for the quality of our lives is not always the most welcomed approach, especially where problems are concerned).

ACTIVITY: Instruct the students to mark an X through the number of the rules that they find hardest to believe and explain why. Circle the number of the rules that give them the most hope and that they have a feeling that it/they are true. Again, explain why.

Facilitator should give an example of each from their own life as an example for the class.

* * * * *

Needless to say, a lesson was never just a one class period. Too, each class progressed at different rates, and there was no way for me to predict the time it would take. Since I wasn't teaching an academic course there was no pressure on me to cover material; therefore, I never rushed a discussion or limited any activity that was taking longer than I had anticipated.

Another major objective for this course was to provide my students with an awareness of the role their thoughts play in creating their reality. I gave this lesson much thought and lots of preparation went into creating a unit of study that would get their attention and make believers out of them. Of course, knowing and doing are two different things, but at least I could expose them to the facts and then the rest was up to them. I wonder if my life would have been lived differently had someone taught me as a teenager that I was the architect of my life, and I built it one thought at a time?

* * * * *

LESSON OBJECTIVE: To understand that whatever we are feeling is what we are vibrating, and whatever we are vibrating is what we are attracting.

INTRODUCTORY SCRIPT: Our feelings are one of our greatest resources. This is true because, "Every feeling you have about your life (no matter how slight) goes to create the events that are coming to you." Lynn Grabhorn, author of *Excuse Me, Your Life Is Waiting.*

Thought precedes feelings. Then, our feelings create our attitudes, that are then evidenced in our behaviors. And, THOUGHT, like everything else in the universe, is some intensity of energy. Allow the students to consider the theory that we attract the events/situations in our lives. (A correct answer isn't required here).

ACTIVITY ONE: Lead a class discussion on the following questions. Obviously, there are no correct/incorrect answers.

The value of this exercise is to get the students to begin thinking about the part their feelings play in their drama.

1. Who thinks that their feelings are the enemy?
2. How much time do you spend experiencing emotions you don't want?
3. Who believes that they 'can't help how they feel'?
4. Do you judge your feelings as good or bad? Why?
5. Have you been told that you shouldn't feel certain ways? What is your reaction to that directive?
6. What is your reaction to the idea that 'our feelings are a very powerful resource in our life'?
7. Do girls have more feelings than boys? If so, is this the way it should be?
8. Do you try to bury your feelings when they are labeled as inappropriate by society?

FACILITATOR SCRIPT: Did you know..............from *Excuse Me, Your Life Is Waiting*

"Everything in this world is made of energy: you, me, the rock, the table, our THOUGHTS, your tennis shoes? And since energy is actually vibration, that means that everything that exists vibrates. Everything! Including you and me.

Modern-day physicists have finally come to agree that energy and matter are one and the same, which brings us back to where we started: that everything vibrates, because everything (whether you can see it or not) is energy. Pure, pulsing, ever-flowing energy. But even though there's only one energy, it vibrates differently. Just like the sound that pours out of a musical instrument, some energy vibrates fast (such as high notes) from high frequencies, and some vibrates slowly (such as low notes) from low frequencies. Unlike the tones from a musical instrument, however, the energy that flows out from us comes from our highly charged emotions to create highly charged electromagnetic wave patterns of energy, making us powerful, but volatile, walking magnets.

So whether it's high vibrational joy, or low vibrational worry, what we are vibrationally offering in any moment is what we are attracting back. We are the initiators of the vibrations, therefore the magnets, the cause. Like it or not, we have created - and are creating - it all. We may be flesh and blood, but first and foremost we are energy, and magnetic energy at that. This makes us living, breathing magnets. SO ONCE AGAIN: Our feelings go out from us in electromagnetic waves. Whatever frequency goes out will automatically attract its identical frequency, thus causing things to happen - good or bad - by finding their matching vibrations. Yes, as we think, we feel; as we feel, we vibrate; as we vibrate, we attract."

As you already realize, our thoughts may be automatic and we may even be unconscious of them, but nevertheless, (as was mentioned when we were considering the quote for this lesson), feelings follow thought. Then we develop attitudes that are the result of how we are feeling. Then these attitudes show themselves in our behavior. Consequently, our reality is the end result of our thoughts. Of course, people share a common reality (this room, time, place), but that isn't the only reality. We all have our own individual (relative) reality, the one that is being produced by our thoughts this very minute (give examples of relative reality using the present moment).

FACILITATOR'S CLOSING SCRIPT: from Peter Rosen's, *The Luminous Life*

"It has been said that, "No one knows enough to be a pessimist." We are living in the age of information. There is so much to know about every subject under the sun - and more to come that we can't even dream of now. Therefore, if what you have just seen seems 'hard to believe', this is not a problem. That's fine. As long as you can halt the 'that is the craziest thing I've ever seen' thoughts and maintain an open mind and give yourself permission to consider new information, that fosters new understanding and insight. You see...............we exist in the physical world, but we control from within."

"The western world that we live in has been fed the 'Big Lie'. That life is filled with limits. That it is a struggle. That there is nothing beyond logic. If, however, you and I are willing to undertake a complete change in how we THINK......thus.....FEEL.....then our lives will reflect a power and greater control over our physical world. There is no separation between any living thing and the SOURCE (give IT any name that fits for you). Science now knows that all of creation is a part of the unified field (the astronaut's demo showed how this can be seen). And, as a result of this business of everything being an aspect of the ONE, we, as spiritual beings, can access this INVISIBLE INTELLIGENCE. We do this with our thoughts, that create the feelings that show in our attitudes and behavior. So, if our level of self awareness is such that we buy this 'possibility' for how things are set up, then we have to re-educate ourselves, if we want to do a better job of living our life. Man is a mental being. And, there is no other bondage than the habit of our uninvestigated thoughts."

* * * * *

Easily the most popular subject for our class time together had to do with love relationships. I was sure that every one of my students was either so in love that they couldn't think straight, or they were in mortal dread of losing the object of their affection, or they were broken up and filled with pain, anger, regret, or revenge. Therefore, my attempt to get them to understand that it was the way they were thinking about their own personal situation that needed to be investigated, took weeks. Even so, some of the students wouldn't change. They preferred their familiar misery to taking responsibility for their thoughts that were causing their suffering. I introduced them to Bryon Katie's process for inquiring into their thoughts by using the four questions that would show them if the thought was true or not. I knew going in that you can lead a horse to water, but you can't make it drink. Nevertheless, I loved the attempt and remembered not to look for results. I just gave it my best shot every day, knowing that the teacher always learns more than the student, and for sure, I needed daily reminders of what I knew to be the practical ways to live my life consciously.

* * * * *

LESSON OBJECTIVE: To demonstrate the four question inquiry method of Bryon Katie's so that each student could, if they chose, learn the habit of investigating their troubling thoughts and not just accept them as truth. This entire lesson is taken from Bryon Katie's *The Work*.

QUOTES: "It's not your job to understand me - it's mine." Bryon Katie, author of *Loving What Is*

"I need your love..........is that true?" Bryon Katie

INTRODUCTORY SCRIPT: Do you operate on the theory that if only the other person understood you, all would be fine? What do you do to understand your own thoughts? Do you act as though they are true simply because you thought them? Hurt feelings or discomfort of any kind cannot be caused by another person. That's not a possibility. It's only when I believe a stressful thought that I get hurt. And I'm the one who's hurting me by believing what I think. This is very good news, because it means that I don't have to get someone else to stop hurting me. I'm the one who can stop hurting me. It's within my power. What we are doing with inquiry is meeting our thoughts with some simple understanding. Finally, pain, anger, and frustration will let us know when it's time to inquire. We either believe what we think or we question it; there's not another choice. Questioning our thoughts is the kinder way.

FIRST CLASS ACTIVITY:

1. Read the following story to the class, "The Oatmeal Man".

The first time a certain young man slept over at his girlfriend's apartment, she served him her favorite breakfast: oatmeal. He didn't mention that he hated oatmeal, because he didn't want any disagreement between them, especially after they'd just had sex. He didn't question the thought that telling her the truth would displease her. After they got married, she often served him oatmeal, and he continued to eat it. He thought that if he admitted his loathing for oatmeal now, he would displease her even more, since it would reveal that he'd been dishonest for a long time. He would rather eat oatmeal than face what he believed his wife would think of him if he told her the truth. And oatmeal is what he is still eating for breakfast, twenty three years later.

2. Ask the students to think about what they do for love that they wouldn't otherwise do. Give them time to write them down on their handout. Then have the students, silently, pretend/imagine reading each item to their partner and asking, "Has it worked? Is this what you love?"

3. Divide the class into small groups of no more than four students. Instruct them to discuss their realizations about what they do for love.

SECOND CLASS ACTIVITY: Assign the following role plays to be read by different students. Follow each role-play with a discussion of the truth that was revealed by doing Bryon Katie's inquiry process on each situation.

FIRST ROLE PLAY

"If you love me, you'll do what I want"

FACILITATOR INTRODUCTION: Horses grazing in a field unthinkingly stand head to tail, flicking the flies from each other's faces. At night, they sleep standing up, resting their heads on each other's withers. This is what peaceful reciprocation looks like. But 'civilized' people have learned how to use reciprocation to torture each other. All it takes is the belief that if I do something for you, you owe me something in return. If I give you my love, you'd better give me yours, or something of equal value.

What happens if you don't reciprocate? I take back my love and approval, and I give you resentment instead. The rules of each relationship dictate all the things you have to do or not do to avoid resentment. These rules aren't written down or even spoken. You find out what they are by breaking them. When you see that I'm angry, you know you've broken a rule. You did something you shouldn't have, you came home too late or too early, you forgot to do or say something. Perhaps you should ask what you did wrong, but watch out. One of the rules may be that you're supposed to know without asking.

If you do your best to figure out all the rules and obey them, do you get my love? No. You get to tiptoe around me, so that you can minimize my anger and continue the relationship. Love seems to have disappeared. Where did it go? You can find out by questioning the thought, "If you love me, you'll do what I want."

If you love me, you'll do what I want. Is it true?

It seems to be.

Can I absolutely know that it's true? What's the reality of it?

No, I can't absolutely know that that's true. The reality of it is that sometimes you don't do what I want.

How do I react when I believe the thought "If you love me, you'll do what I want"?

I assess everything you do for me and everything I do for you in terms of its exchange value. I keep a score sheet on our relationship to measure how much love you are giving me. I make lists of demands that I present to you in an aggrieved manner, saying or implying that I'll love you only if you deliver on my list. And I make other lists of what you would do if you really loved me. I present these to you angrily or use them internally as proof that you don't love or appreciate me. I withdraw from you, using your infractions, your failure to deliver, as my reason for the separation I inflict. I withhold sex. I don't give you what I secretly want to give you, and I feel a lot of shame and guilt about that, and then I hate myself and begin to overeat, smoke and drink too much, and I justify my actions by blaming you for being so unfair. I get angry at you when I feel lonely or empty, thinking that if only you had done what I wanted, I wouldn't have to feel this way. I usually end up thinking that you don't love me.

Who would I be if I didn't believe the thought "If you love me, you'll do what I want"? What if that thought just passed through my mind like air?

I would look at you without keeping score. I wouldn't concern myself with whether something you've done means that you love me or not. If you didn't do what I want, it would be fine with me. I would understand why you didn't do it and why that was right for you in that moment, and if I didn't understand, I could ask you. I wouldn't take it personally. I would remain calm and happy. If what I wanted you to do for me was something I could do myself, I would simply do it. Without the thought "If you loved me, you'd do what I want," I would come back to myself. I would notice that I love you, and then continue with my own activities. It would be like not having you in my life except as someone I love and care about. I would be a much calmer and happier person. I would be grateful for you. I would like myself more.

SECOND ROLE PLAY

"I should be his one and only".

I should be his one and only. Is that true?

Well, it's pretty obvious to me that my life would be better.

And can you absolutely know for sure that your life would be better?

No.

How do you react when you believe the thought that he should dump the other girls?

I try to undermine them. I try to convince him to be monogamous. I'm always jealous. I think of them constantly and of his being with them. I constantly compare myself with them. Am I prettier than this one? Am I smarter than that one?

That's a very painful way to live. It's painful to try to manipulate the man you love, to spend your time plotting how you can get rid of people he loves or wondering if you're as good as they are. Whose business is it that he insists on keeping these other girls in his life?

I hate this question.

You hate it because you're holding on to your pain for dear life. You're holding on to your thoughts of "I'm right and he's wrong. I'm the good one and he's the villain." Would you rather be right or at peace?

I'd rather be free and have some peace. I really would. I've had enough of this misery.

So, whose business is it whom he stays romantically involved with?

It's his business. I know that. It's his business, not mine.

And whose business is it whom you are attracted to and want to be with?

It's my business.

He should only love you – is that true? What's the reality of it? He doesn't. He stays involved with other girls. That's the reality of it. It doesn't go along with our morality, it doesn't go along with what society would teach us, it's what is. It's an outright lie that he should only love you, WHEN HE DOESN'T. What happens inside you when you believe the thought that he should love only you?

I hate him.

And how does that feel inside you?

Awful. I just want to die.

And how do you treat him when you believe the thought that he should be faithful to you?

I rage at him. I cut myself off. I close my heart.

Is that pretty painful?

It's horrible.

The reason you experience pain and loneliness is that you're mentally in his business, and it doesn't leave anyone here present with you. Of course you're lonely. She's over there with him, you're over there with him, everyone's over there with him, and there's no one here with you. You think he's supposed to be with you, but you can't even do it. He leaves you, you leave you – what is the difference? The way to stay present is to question your thoughts. "He shouldn't be with other girls" – is that true? "I would be much better off if he were with me and not her" – can you absolutely know that that's true? He's not responsible for your misery, you are. You're believing a lie, and that's what is causing your pain. Can you see a reason to drop this thought that argues with reality, "He should be with only me"?

Yes, I hate to suffer.

I see we come from the same school. And please don't try to drop it. No one can drop a thought. We're just seeing a reason to drop it. Can you see a reason to believe that thought that doesn't hurt?

No.

Who would you be without that thought?

I wouldn't hate him so much. Maybe I wouldn't feel so betrayed. I don't know if I could ever open my heart to him again, but at least I would be more understanding.

An open mind is an open heart. Who knows what you would feel or how you would treat him if you didn't believe your thoughts about him? Who would you be, in his presence, if you didn't believe the thought that he should get rid of his other girlfriends? Close your eyes, picture him with them, look at his face without any belief that he should choose you. Can you see him?

Yes. He is so handsome. He looks happy.

Now that is unconditional love. That is who you really are.

* * * * *

I never knew at the end of a school day if any student really understood me, believed what they had experienced in class, or even if they wanted to. From my own practice, I knew all too well that giving up some painful thought wasn't always what I wanted to do. Crazy as that may be. But, oh how I loved facilitating these classes. I reminded myself often to not look for results. Give it my best shot every day, and be content with that. Besides I was busy enough with myself. With my daily thoughts that needed to be investigated for the truth. This was probably the biggest perk in it for me.

CHAPTER FIVE

January – November, 2001

"It's The Years in The Middle I Can't Do"

From *A Reliable Wife* by Robert Goolrick: "She liked the beginnings of things. The pure white possibility of the empty room, the first kiss. And endings, she liked endings too. The drama of the smashing glass, the tearful goodbye, the last awful word which could never be unsaid or unremembered. It was the middle that gave her pause. She didn't trust the middle."

"December, 1998

Dear Cathy,

I absolutely can't wait to see you. I am so jazzed about our upcoming 1999 festivities. It will be wonderful to have you here. Naturally, I am using the 'coming attractions' as the perfect reason to finish buying the few items needed to make the house look complete. You know, little things like a coffee table, end tables, and decorator items. Your dad is doing very well with this attack of 'home beautiful'. It's nothing close to a car show, but he does play his part. Anyway, it will be wonderful to have you and Hilda here a few days after Christmas. You may want to know that we are adding one little activity to the New Year festivities. Brian and I are going to get married on Jan. 2, and we hope you'll *be happy about this. How we are going to do this is subject to change, at this time, but I think that we will get married here at home, follow the ceremony with a cocktail party reception, then begin the celebration of Hilda's 90th birthday by moving the party to a wonderful restaurant for dinner, champagne, cake and dancing. Your dad and I are researching what Houston has to offer (This is the fun part...........getting dressed up on a Saturday night, going to a different place, testing the food and atmosphere). The guest list includes my three children and their families, my brother and his wife (Hilda loves them), my favorite uncle, two very close female friends of ours and you. Attire is glitter and glitz. Think sparkle! Hilda is going to bring something she has, but we plan to shop here for the perfect dress if she wants to. And she will. Must run. It is time to feed your dad again. I have a million things to tell you and I want to hear about your life too. My plan is to send the other family members to bed and we can then have a late-night summit on New Year's Eve. Love ya, Bonn"*

Our wedding on January 2, 1999 wasn't the beginning for me. It felt more like the middle of our relationship. I guess that was to be expected since we had already lived together for three years. Nevertheless, the passion and romance one associates with a wedding day was missing for me. I wasn't surprised or bothered by it, but I do wonder if Brian realized that the hug and my 'I'm so tired I can't move' excuse on our wedding night alerted him to coming attractions. And, even though I didn't like to admit it, my decision to marry had more to do with our future life than it did with the feeling that 'I can't live without you'. At least, from my side of the fence. I don't really know what was true for Brian. After all, I was the one to suggest we marry. I would, years later, use this fact as evidence that he lets the woman in his life call the shots for him. True enough, he wanted me to repay my teacher retirement so we could have a larger collective retirement fund, and to do this he had to pay for more of our current living expenses. But did he really love me or did he too look at the financial wisdom of us being married as the main motivation for the ceremony? It would be the last year of his life before I would know the answer to that question.

My nights and weekends were now the point of my life, not teaching school. My book, *Higher Ground, One Woman's Journey*, was being edited, the art teacher at ALC was designing the cover, and I was getting very close to having this writing project I had started in 1992 completed. However, it wasn't until the truck pulled up in front of my house and unloaded boxes and boxes of books into the three car garage that panic took over. What in the world had I been thinking? I would have to sell all these books, and I don't remember ever thinking about that aspect of becoming a published author. Was it possible that I really hadn't thought about that? If so, I am guilty of being compulsive and not thinking things through. Or maybe, this 'not giving any major life decision enough thought' is the reason my life is not as neat and tidy as those of most friends and family. But good lord, what do I do now?

I armed myself with John Kremer's book, *1001 Ways to Market Your Books*, and I followed his every word. The third bedroom that was my office was where I lived every day after school. Brian was a sweetheart to let me work at this marketing thing for hours at a time during the week, and then to spend every weekend going to book events in Houston, Hallettsville, College Station, and Austin. I did enjoy talking to people about the book, and I was selling them, but how long would I be so interested and motivated to keep at it? I have been known to have a short attention span, and this had me worried.

Life in Houston, in our new home, had taken on a comfortable routine. My teaching life at ALC was going smoothly, and I never dreaded going to work. If only Brian's had been as enjoyable, but he didn't complain much. Sure, he told the day's horror stories at dinner, but usually with a sense of humor. His heart going in and out of rhythm did affect his energy level and peace of mind, but it wasn't anything that interfered with his life noticeably. We settled into habits that suited us both.

I went to jazzercise religiously right after school; made dinner, then disappeared into my office until bedtime. Brian kept his Mustang convertible ready to compete at the local car shows, washed the dishes, and then read his car magazines until bedtime. Weekends were spent either going to car shows and book events, to Hallettsville to visit my family, or driving down to Galveston in the convertible. Spring slipped into summer and our travels. Unlike his other wives, I had encouraged Brian to be more involved with his daughters, and this pleased me as much as it did him. Chris, her husband and new baby girl came to visit us in Houston, and we went to see them in New Jersey during the summer. Cathy was single and I just loved her life there close to Washington DC. The day we toured the Smithsonian nearly killed me. My legs have never been so tired, but oh what a glorious day! And, of course, we had Hilda come for several weeks to visit us in Houston. I have never known anyone who could shop all day, every day and never tire of it. There was no way Brian would agree to be a part of it, so I would drive her to a different shopping mall every day, listen to her squeal with excitement over 'this darlin' dress, and then still be filled with energy when she hit the door with her new purchases to show Brian the day's choices. I couldn't get aggravated with her, nor did Brian. How could anyone fault someone who took so much pleasure in the day, and she never uttered one negative word. Anywhere I took her; any thing I made for dinner; any kind of cocktail offered, it didn't matter. Scarlet loved it all. Especially when I called her Scarlet, instead of Hilda.

Yes, life was to my liking, in every way. Just give me more to do than is humanly possible, cross country travel on a regular basis, the interaction of a larger family now scattered in four different states, and a teaching job that made every day an adventure. A nice, comfortable home with a husband who never interfered with my day and often times even added to it. So by first anniversary time, I was beginning to believe that my son Jon was wrong when he had proclaimed, years earlier, that I was not marriage material. We celebrated at the Steakhouse in Moulton, TX where my daughter's wedding dinner and dance had been held. I did get Brian to dance with me, but we were not the main attraction. Hilda and my son Jon were the night's dancers! Was that woman really 91 years old, was the unasked question in the eyes of all the guests. Her eyes were sparkling as they whirled their way around the dance floor. Definitely, she was in love with Jon by the end of the evening.

I suppose that because the year 2000 was so lacking in trauma/drama, 2001 caught me off guard. The fact that I began the year sick, and continued to be into April, evidence enough that I had moved from placid waters to life altering turbulence. Had my now past years of smoking finally caught up with me? One doctor looked at the Xray and quickly and definitely announced that I had emphysema. Nevertheless, as I battled the Houston traffic to tell Brian, I felt very threatened by this news, but at the same time I had the feeling that somehow it didn't fit. So, of course we got a second opinion, and sure enough there was some evidence of asthma, but nothing getting out of the polluted Houston air couldn't remedy. And, that was just what I wanted to hear. I could retire in May because I now had my Texas Teacher Retirement fund repaid. Too, after my visit during spring break to see my sister, LaVoyce, who now lived in Santa Fe, NM, I was feeling the pull to go west again. We had just sold our home and had moved into Cameron's garage apartment, so relocating could be quick and easy. Brian wouldn't be a problem either because he loved the western states as much as I did. Too, how often had we both taken the geographic cure for what ailed us? No, Brian wasn't the problem. My 'Oh God, no' musings around wishing I was single again, was the problem.

Brian hadn't done anything wrong. Brian wasn't any different now than he was before we married. No, it is the same ole story that always features Bonn the compulsive bride. Not counting my first marriage to the father of my children, the scenario is this: I marry men who love me. My reasons vary. I find them (within a very brief period of time) lovable, nice looking, and of good character. Or my financial future would be well served if I had a husband. Then, as the years go by, I find that the life we have together bores me to death, and they fail to meet my needs. You know, the ones I dismissed as unimportant, when I married them. Additionally, I am not candid with them because I do not reveal how I am feeling. Instead, I find fault, and then I leave. From the metaphysical perspective all my physical ailments thus far this year of 2001: laryngitis, bronchitis, upper respiratory infection, fluid in my left ear, and now the diagnosis of asthma, point to not expressing my emotions. When will I get it? I teach it. I believe it. Nevertheless, I can't live it consistently. I caution myself to not get so emotionally involved with my disappointment with Brian and give this marriage a chance. Please God! I pray I wasn't premature to declare my son Jon wrong about me not being marriage material.

It was the season of 'The Weddings'. Cathy's wedding in May was the first of the two summertime family weddings. It followed the fabulous, formal to the max, Florida beach wedding in March of my step niece, Jennifer. Cathy's wedding was held in a beautiful hotel resort in the Washington DC area. All was perfectly executed, and Brian could not have been more proud of his beautiful daughter.

The groom's family, being Vietnamese, added dimensions to everything, from the food to the conversation. Hilda was our roommate, thus I got to enjoy her perspective on everything. The fact that we almost missed our plane because I was in the emergency room was the only trauma of the entire weekend. However, as it turned out, the spring pollen in the air in that eastern state, that caused my asthmatic reaction, was the catalyst for getting us out of Houston. My doctor recommended that, if possible, we should move to a less polluted environment. Four days later Brian resigned, and we started planning our move back to Arizona. Cameron was sorry to see us go, but she was more interested in my current understanding of Brian, our relationship, and me. Having lived around us for the past five months, she knew how challenged I was to be content with my marriage.

"Like you and me and everyone else, Brian is a product of his childhood," I explained. It was a warm spring Saturday by the pool, and Cameron and I had it all to ourselves. "Because of his mother, Brian was set up to always have a woman in his life wanting him to be something he wasn't. He was a boy, not a girl. Hilda was so into apparel and appearance that she dressed him British style with knickers, suspenders, knee socks and bow tie. Needless to say, the American kids were brutal, and he developed asthma. Thank goodness the family doctor had sense enough to realize the problem and had her stop it. Next, the mother of his children wanted more from him than he was willing to give. It was the decade of the liberated woman, so why in the world couldn't he help with house work, or at least be her assistant when entertaining? Add to that the fact that rural life didn't fit her any longer, thus the college sweetheart days turned into marital discontent."

"That's what gets me about marriage. One cannot predict what the years will do to the beginning plans and agreements, but do continue," Cameron interjected with a wry smile.

"Well, wife number two traveled because of her job. Brian told me that she would hit the house on Fridays and instantly get upset if leaves were on the walk, or the dishes were draining. His housekeeping didn't suit her at all. And it seems that when they were dating, she had pretended to love camping, but he soon discovered that was fake. Her campaign to get him to end his passion for the great outdoors set the stage for divorce court. But would you believe that his third wife wanted to do nothing but camping and she demanded lots more sex. Sorry to say, that by then, Brian was not as interested in either any more."

"Damn, this story is scary," laughed Cameron. "There isn't any way anyone can win in this marriage thing. But do tell me what you demand of poor Brian that doesn't happen."

"Oh I win the prize! All I want is for him to embrace the spiritual approach to life. You know, the way I do. Come on Brian, be conscious about how you think. And for goodness sakes, don't insist that others are responsible for your happiness, and above all, read all the spiritual growth books I have in every room, and meditate, of course."

Cameron looked at me with a puzzled smile on her face. "You know something, Bonn? You are the only person I know who can poke fun at what you obviously believe and take so seriously. I don't get it."

"It's a curse," I laughed. "I see myself too clearly, and I'm not sure there is any advantage to that because I don't seem to benefit greatly. One would think that I could recast myself into this peaceful, grateful, mature woman who is accepting of myself and what life brings. But no, instead I stuff the thoughts that go unexamined for their truth until I have had enough, then I start thinking about leaving. Obviously, one of the reasons I prefer being single is that I like myself more that way. I'm not nearly as critical of myself when I'm not married." Laughter signaled the end of our summit by the pool. I started getting up to go into our garage apartment to start dinner, so Cameron got in the last word. "All you need to do, Bonn, is remember what Gail (our mutual Houston psychic) told you years ago. Don't give them so many jobs. Decide on a couple of things you want most from your guy. Is it good sex, mucho money, intellectual conversation or knock-down-dead good looks? Then, let the other essentials go."

Cameron couldn't see the smile on my face as I opened the door to my apartment. I was considering mentioning that Gail didn't say a word about the 'being in love' thing. I decided against it, and waved goodbye. What was the point? One was either a big fan of 'being in love' or you weren't. From experience I could attest to the fact that those love feelings get a relationship started, but since they don't last, they haven't been the glue that has kept me in a marriage.

If Jennifer and Cathy's weddings were outstanding for their elegance and obvious detailed planning, my sister LaVoyce's son Mike's, won the prize for being the most relaxed, informal, and infectious with a holiday spirit. He and his bride, Rachel, chose Ouray, CO for its primitive beauty and casual atmosphere. On the weekend of May 24th, there among the majestic mountains and pioneer citizens of Ouray, gathered many friends and family from all over the country. As Brian and I drove into Colorado, I noticed his singing with the radio and whistling with instrumentals. Obviously, happiness was renewing his spirit. Nothing made him angry, not even when our trip was delayed a couple of hours because of a bicycle race. We just got out of our car and took a hike. Now that we had a defined plan to move back to Arizona, we were both in a better frame of mind. I suppose it was the ole geographic cure thing again, but as long as I didn't analyze him, me, or our relationship………it was good medicine.

When we pulled in at 2pm the day of the wedding, everyone was already there. My son Lyle, LaVoyce and her son Murray and ex-husband Tom, waved us a welcome. Tom's sister, Pud and her husband, Tom's daughter

Michelle, with her family from California were in attendance. Friends from their college days, hometown friends, and Texas family were eating hamburgers and playing baseball. Brian jumped right in. He ate better than usual and then headed for the baseball field. All went well until a twelve year old kid struck him out. Thankfully, he didn't get mad. He just couldn't believe it.

As the afternoon progressed, some of us ladies left the picnic to do some decorating at the church. Because Rachel was cool with whatever anyone wanted to do, LaVoyce and I found our way to the historic church and arranged some flowers here and there on the pews and in the altar area. Actually, four people getting dressed in the one room took more planning. And, there were challenges. Lyle had forgotten his suit, therefore he had to wear casual clothes with a pair of Brian's more appropriate shoes. The sink in the bathroom was in such a confined space that Brian had to bend down to shave. The Beaumont Hotel was historic, but not necessarily guest friendly. The two double beds for four large bodies would be a challenge. Hopefully, by bedtime we would all be so tired and full of food and drink that we wouldn't notice.

LaVoyce was elegant in the long, slim, red skirt with a Spanish pepper sequined top I had provided. Now that she was so thin, she turned everyone's head. She was just beautiful, and Tom's eyes revealed sad regret concerning their lives now after divorce. LaVoyce told me, after the ceremony, that Tom had congratulated her on how she had raised their sons as he sat next to her at the wedding. Then he danced with her one time later that evening, and that was it. No words between them. The usual way people live the first years after divorce.

I had never seen Rachel with her long hair up and wearing makeup. She was stunning in her ivory wedding dress that flowed to the floor in an unruffled, soft way. Everyone could see that Mike's reaction to his bride walking down the aisle was a mixture of pride, love, and amazement. During the traditional ceremony, the only person standing before the altar that was in a strain was Murray. He was very sick with an upper respiratory infection. Actually, the only thing that had him standing there beside his brother as best man was the shot he had gotten that afternoon when his mom and I interrupted our church decorating to rush him to the doctor.

The dinner and dance was held at a state park a few miles out of Ouray. Such memories!! To begin with, Mike's friend who was driving right ahead of them, was stopped by the state police for speeding. Brian and I were shocked to see Rachel, the bride, standing beside the road while the police were deciding whether or not to let Mike's friend off. Seems he was driving without a license, and Mike was trying to influence the officer to let him go and not fine him. Begrudgingly the policeman finally did, and the story was the first to make the rounds among the guests at the park pavilion. It was a grand place. Covered, made of rock, and multi level. The band had the perfect place to set up under the stars on the adjoining, round dance floor. The weather was perfect for being outside, and after a marvelous meal, everyone moved over to the dance area to either observe or dance.

Brian did the best he could, but since Lyle was there, I had a great dance partner. In the early 1990's when he had been a student at Emery Riddle Aeronautical University in Prescott, AZ and I was living in Sedona, we had taught country dance lessons at the university. So, naturally we had to show off a bit. But, when Mike and Rachel came back on the floor in their shorts and sandals for travel to a remote island off the coast of Panama, they stole the show. Rachel still had on her bridal veil with her shorts and Tshirt. Mike twirled her around to a spirited song as the guests cheered and clapped. Only Tom, Lyle, and Murray were battling cheerless feelings. Tom, my sister's ex-husband, would be returning to an empty apartment to continue his life alone in a new town. Lyle, my youngest son, would be returning to a very Spartan life as a soon-to-graduate massage therapist in Scottsdale, AZ. And Murray, LaVoyce's oldest son, would be returning to the US Air Force top gun training where it was against military rules to date a student pilot he was attracted to.

As we said our goodbyes to everyone and headed back toward Texas, I was very aware of all my many blessings. Brian and I were doing very well together. Travel had always agreed with us. Days of sightseeing; romantic nights in strange towns along our route, and conversation that revolved around our moving plans to Arizona. But most importantly, oh how I was sleeping these days. As we drove along, I would fade off, time and again. While Brian was shopping for shirts and hats, and taking hours to make a selection, instead of getting mad, I would just take a nap in the car. After all, it's a matter of perspective. I congratulated myself for remembering.

Earlier during this spring of 2001, while waiting my turn in a doctor's office, I had noticed an advertisement for Westbrook University, a distance learning institution. They offered a PhD in Transpersonal Psychology, and when I stopped flipping the pages in the magazine and read the ad, a bell went off in my head. My favorite psychic, Sean Harribance, had all but commanded me to get my PhD last year. He told me in a very emphatic way that I was behind schedule. I should already have it. His exact words were, "If you want to live well into your 90's, you must get this highest degree and then pursue your destiny. If you do not, you will die."

"And my destiny is?" I had asked in a joking way.

"You will know. Pay attention to your guide. She communicates with you through your thoughts. Get the degree. It will give you the credentials you need to do whatever it is you are meant to do."

After braving the task of sharing this prediction and the advertisement with Brian, much to my relief, he was okay with this development in my life. Therefore, we took a quick trip to New Mexico so I could meet with the president of the school. I wanted to be very sure I was getting an education before I signed up and laid my thousands down. After she showed me around the school, she talked to me at length about a degree in Transpersonal Psychology.

"This degree is a study of human consciousness beyond the personal dimension, including the paranormal. Emotions, creativity, art, metaphysics, wellness and parapsychology are major themes of study."

I could hardly contain myself. These were the very topics I had had so much interest in for years. My constant reading was almost exclusively related, and my book, *Higher Ground, One Woman's Journey,* was narrative nonfiction. This happened by accident. Instead of writing a 'how to' book about spiritual growth, I told my stories about my journey, and as I spun my true tales, I would slip in the practical spiritual psychology that related to the episodes and incidents of my life. And now I discover that there is actually a degree I can earn in this field! Good heavens, I didn't even know it was a 'field'.

Since we were in New Mexico, naturally we stopped in Santa Fe to visit my sister LaVoyce on our way back to Abilene, TX where my granddaughter Megan would be competing in the State Championship Barrel Racing Contest. From all accounts, LaVoyce was beginning to live her new life very well. It had taken her several weeks to get past the unpacked boxes that filled the unlighted living room of her new apartment on Zia Road. Looking for a job, furnishing her new space, and finding her way around Santa Fe were tremendous challenges for her. But the initial paralyzing inertia of those first few weeks was now gone. She was unpacked and her darling apartment was evidence of her decorating ability. She had braved the winter cold to go door to door in downtown Santa Fe looking for work, and had found a position with a well known law firm. And, she certainly looked the part these days of the professional single woman making her way in the world. I had never known her to take as much interest in her clothes as now. Thank goodness I no longer needed my professional clothes, and they fit her perfectly. Anyone looking at her in The Bull Ring, where I met her for lunch, would conclude that she had the world by the tail. However, knowing my sister the way I did gave me pause. This new life of her's, after being married for decades, was not what she would have ordered for herself. LaVoyce was best suited to having a man in her life, to running a luxurious home and mothering two boys, and to navigating the Denver social scene. Unlike me, she had no self-imposed demand to achieve. She thrived on long, slow, summer days at their cabin out of Creede, Co, where she filled her hours with helping her little boys fish, decorating the cabin with her original art, touring the beautiful countryside in a jeep with John LaFont, a Creede oldtimer and the 'little fellars' and going into town on a Saturday night to dance and drink with the locals.

LaVoyce and I were not alike in any way. No one ever took us for sisters. I was taller, with short, casual blond hair, consistently slim without much effort, and although I knew I was attractive, LaVoyce was the family beauty. She was ravishing with her shoulder-length, chestnut hair; her sexy body that was always being subjected to yet another diet, and those eyes of hers that hinted at bedroom lure. Emotionally we were different too. Being the middle child, and the second girl, LaVoyce grew up without the love and attention she needed from Daddy. Consequently, a man's love became her pursuit in adult life. However, my reaction to our childhood created in me a person who does not necessarily value a man's love. It would be impossible to count the number of times my sister and I have debated the question as to which of us is to be the more pitied. The one who has explained her self defeating behavior in the name of love, or the one who has lived to lament the fact that not being in love with her husband made living the marriage something to escape.

My granddaughter Megan, now twelve years old, was the reason we began our trip west to find our home in Arizona. Such fun we all had the first three days in June at this state barrel racing competition in Abilene, TX. Megs, on her horse Dandy, ran a 16.600 to qualify for the finals. Nevertheless, because she knocked over the third barrel during the finals, her 16.323 time didn't count. Everyone was disappointed, but her not winning didn't keep us from having a great time together. This was the first of three more annual state and world championship contests that Brian and I would attend. Always, it was a memorable time for both happy and hair raising reasons. What we ate and where, was a daily highlight. Ross, my son-in-law, could be depended on to guide us to the best steak houses in Abilene and the best seafood restaurants in Jackson, Mississippi. Actually, quality family time revolved around this hobby of Megan's. It would be until after her graduation from high school before any other interest took precedence over barrel racing. It was an extended family affair with the mix of both my sons, granddaughter Cody, the father of my children, and other Hallettsville relatives providing the cheering section for many local and state runs. However, a month later in July, only Brian and I were present for the traumatic fall she took in Jackson, Mississippi at the world competition.

Her new horse, Big John, had years of experience and came highly recommended. Since Megan's legs were getting longer and longer, her favorite horse Dandy needed to be replaced with this larger one. It scared me to see Megan on him. He was so fast, and she didn't have the control of him that she had exercised with Dandy. Therefore, when he cut the third barrel so close, her left knee hit the barrel and it threw her backward and out of the saddle. Big John stopped instantly and this action on the part of this well trained horse saved her from being dragged or stepped on. Ross was running to her as the announcer was commenting on how well behaved Big John was. I aged ten years, but Megan was not hurt. The announcer was so sweet and he got a chuckle from the large crowd when he said, "Now don't you worry one bit about that, little lady. Everyone knows you can't call yourself a cowgirl until you've been dusted."

Then, because of this mishap, I have a favorite memory I'll always cherish. Her parents, Summer and Ross, were completely destroyed with fear of what might have happened, and concern over whether or not this hobby was too dangerous for their only daughter. I suggested that Megs come with us to our motel room for the night. She wanted to, so we walked the distance to the motel, arm in arm. Brian trailed behind us in silence. Megan was dirty, but she didn't want to take a bath. I didn't insist. Instead, I helped her into one of my nightshirts; we crawled into one of the two queen beds together; Brian took our picture to add a visual to this never-to-be-forgotten event, and then my granddaughter curled up in a tight ball to sleep. Of course, I had to ask her one more time if she was okay.

"Yeah, Granny. I'm not hurt. Really, after I got my breath back, the dirt felt cool and I liked that." She was soon fast asleep.

The middle of June found Brian and I looking for a home in or close around Sedona, AZ. Sadly our earlier high hopes and mutual enjoyment of each other were on the wane. The camper trailer next to the water near Page Springs was the perfect setting for love and romance. Nevertheless, because I was having trouble policing my thoughts about Brian's way of showing up for our days of searching for the right place to rent, I was creating unhappy days for myself. Three days ago he started voicing his grievances-against-the-world habit. When we were driving between Cottonwood and Sedona he railed against how all the new highway construction was ruining the natural beauty of the red rocks. Then the next night, while shopping for groceries, he made it miserable for me by insisting on the cheapest price of everything we needed. Naturally, I knew intellectually that these behaviors meant that he was unhappy and fearful about something, but since he was conditioned to trying to please, he didn't say what he was thinking. And, what do I do? I see my thoughts about him as justified, and without sharing my complaints with him, I make him responsible for my growing unhappiness. I was remembering my list of his shortcomings: never any introspective conversation; his infernal slowness (I wait while he takes 20 minutes to eat a bowl of cereal); his stopping to talk to strangers who aren't interested in the subject matter (I wait silently and sullenly a few steps away); me doing more than my share to get something accomplished during the day, and his poverty mentality. Gone in me was any desire to take a perspective that would take him out of the 'you-are-driving-me-crazy' mode. Nope! It was back to sleepless nights, and doubts around wanting to stay married to him.

Thank goodness Lynde, my teacher friend from Hallettsville, woke us up at 4:30 am with a 'what's up' call from Texas. Brian dressed faster than I had ever seen him, and he slammed out of the Little Daisy Motel in Cottonwood before I could tell Lynde that we were fine. He returned from his long walk a man who had something to say.

"I want to talk to you, Bonn. There are things I need to say to you."

He wasn't angry so I was immediately hopeful that this was going to be good.

"I thought we had the same vision about the life we wanted here when we left Houston to return to Arizona. But no. We have been looking at expensive, small, cramped, no-yard condos in Sedona. I need to be out in nature. I want a place where I can fiddle around with cars and do some woodworking too. Is your 'having to be in Sedona' the most important thing to you? Couldn't we look for some more rural place around Clarkdale or here in Cottonwood?"

Now, this was what I needed and wanted. A husband who was willing to be straight with me and tell me what was on his mind. I felt we had turned a page in our relationship and instantly my spirits were renewed.

"I'm sure we can and that will be fine with me. Let's check the newspaper over breakfast and see what perfect place is waiting for us." My kiss told him all was forgiven and that I was genuinely pleased with his declarations.

And, perfect it was! A large, single-story house right on the Verde River, yet inside the city limits of Clarkdale. The kitchen had a section of an old bowling alley from Jerome as the eating bar. Three bedrooms and two baths gave me a room for my office, and the living room was facing the river. The picture window let in the majestic beauty of the willows along the river's edge; the high brown bluff on the other side where eagles would swoop in to look for fish swimming down stream, and the rushing blue water that could be heard from the large patio at night. It was a cool place. A place where the joys of living in Arizona were infectious. After Lyle, my son in Scottsdale, helped us move in, the summer days began to move towards fall. I would stand at the kitchen window and watch Brian clear the area that bordered the river. It had been allowed to grow up, thus we didn't have an easy path to the water, and I had become addicted to at least one dip in the Verde daily. He wasn't being bothered with his heart going in and out of rhythm, and being Farmer Brown in the sunshine daily, had him looking like the Greek god who had rescued me that snowy day in Munds Park back in 1995. Yep, once again I was tempted to hope in the 'and they lived happily ever after' possibility. All the necessary ingredients were in place. My friends from my 1990's life in Sedona were frequent dinner guests (Clark-my Sedona housemate, Mercedes-my real estate friend, Ryan-my favorite dance partner, and even my ex-husband Geof's daughter-in-law). A new business venture for myself that involved creating workshops for teachers of at-risk students, kept me busy in my office during the day. I knew myself well enough to know that I had to have something to do with my time. I had read about, and had longed for the ability to 'stop and smell the roses', but thus far there was little evidence that I would ever be able to manage it. I knew Brian considered this a defect in my personality. And, depending on my mood, I would fault him for not being more like me, the shaker and mover.

I guess it was the parade of peaceful, summer days in a new locale that lulled me into thinking that we were over the hump. I no longer was waiting for the other shoe to drop, and that set me up for total shock when it did. How could a little side trip to a furniture store, after a great weekend at my friend Linda Crosswhite's lovely home in Scottdale, produce such a scene?

It was an antique headboard, and I really wanted it. However, because Brian is a perfectionist, he couldn't appreciate the uniqueness of it because of all the things wrong with it. I could easily tell that he hadn't fallen in love with it the way I had, but I kept pushing. Then, instead of telling me he didn't want to buy it, he took offense to the fact that the salesperson wasn't attentive enough to suit him. All of a sudden, Brian was yelling across the store at the man, and I was wishing for a hole to open up in the floor to swallow me. I was mortified when the manager asked us to leave. That only added to Brian's fury, and for a minute there I feared that the police would be called. By the time we got to the car and headed up the road to Clarkdale, I was in a frenzy, and I found myself talking to him as I would one of my students who had just let their temper get the best of them.

"You act like my ALC students. It is called transference. You obviously didn't like the headboard, but instead of telling me so, you transferred your upset with me to somebody else. The salesclerk was safer than me. You yelled at him because you were upset with me for wanting the headboard."

Brian didn't agree. "He was not being helpful and I was mad at him for being such a piss poor salesman. Don't try using any of your teacher psychology on me. This had nothing to do with you."

"You chose to behave inappropriately, then you blame others for your actions. I wish you could see that in yourself. It isn't exactly a terminal condition. You could change if you wanted to, but first you have to recognize it in yourself." My temper was spent, and I knew there was no point in even talking any longer. I turned on the radio and escaped the moment by thinking about what I could do to help myself. Maybe, just maybe, some of my problem with Brian is that we have been around each other 24/7 for the past three weeks. Beginning tomorrow, I am going to take solo hikes and do lunch more often with my lady friends. I feel sorry for both of us. He tries, I try, but not much changes. Looks like I'll spend the rest of my days thinking that the future is better, thus trying to get disengaged with the present in order to get there. How much time is too much time to spend looking back at what I should not have done, and looking forward to what might yet be? All the gurus tell us that the present is all we have, and I can see the truth in that. Nevertheless, that is not where I live my life regardless of how hard I try to remember that directive.

I don't know why I decided to call two men from years past, but I did. There is something about sitting on that large rock in the river, as the sun is going down, to put me on memory lane. Both were happy to hear from me. Josh, the young student teacher at NAU who was a less-than-wonderful husband in a past life, was full of good news. He has a good teaching job in Michigan, and will be getting married in August. Klint, my almost-husband in the 1980's, reports that he is happy and busy with his life in McAlester,

Oklahoma. He will be potentate of the Shrine in 2003, and his ball will be on April 19. Wish I could be his date for such a grand occasion. What a romantic time we had back in 1994, when he invited me to go to Greg and Linda Schuler's ball. Klint never sounds like he misses me or regrets that we aren't together. In fact, if I talk to him long enough on the phone he gets onto the subject of politics. Seems he and George Bush Jr. worked together years ago in Houston, and Klint is actually going to invite him to his ball. The fact that he is now president of the United States makes no difference. One thing about it, Klint has never suffered from a lack of self esteem. Having worked in Africa, Europe, and Asia in management for Shell Oil Company, has him convinced that he is one of the big boys.

Our new home was the perfect setting for this summer's dinner parties to celebrate birthdays. My son Lyle, and my Sedona and Munds Park ex-housemate Clark's parties were such fun. I especially loved the conversation about several of us taking a road trip together into Mexico for the purpose of finding a hacienda where we could all live together. I know, I just moved here to Arizona, and I'm interested in moving to Mexico with friends and family? It is the 'with friends and family' part that appealed to me. If I had Clark, Mercedes, and Lyle in my daily life, I would be able to stay married to Brian more easily. All three of these people are so good for me. They are all people who live their lives very consciously. For example, last time he visited, Lyle asked me to consider the idea that I am so hard on my mate because I too am a critical person. Sure, this is in my DNA, but blaming Mother doesn't stop me from being like her. My getting upset with the way Brian is so critical is evidence of how critical I am. Never mind that I don't voice it as he does; I think the thoughts. He is a mirror for me. Psychology 101.

It was August and the road trip traveling and visiting family and friends took us from Arizona to Texas, Ohio,

New Jersey, Washington DC, Maryland, New Mexico and Pennsylvania. Taking my granddaughter Cody to see Megan ride at world competition in Jackson, Mississippi was one of the highlights of the trip. She is the easiest child to live around. Being stuffed in the small back seat of Brian's Mustang convertible, with at least twenty books she had checked out to take on the trip, didn't even bother her until we were almost home. My directive to her was to put her mind somewhere else so her cramped long legs wouldn't get so much of her attention. Her response was, "Gran, why do you think I am reading constantly?" I found it interesting that she paid more attention to what the tour guide told us about the antebellum home than any of the rest of us, yet be almost totally unaware of the people and conversation going on around her at the dinner table. For sure, she is an Indigo child who will experience her life more divergently than most.

This time, the geographic cure didn't help much. I didn't enjoy spending my day around Brian. I loved the people we visited; the events we attended, but I found that Brian's thinly veiled temper kept me on edge. So the lady selling the I-Max tickets made a mistake; the Burger King employee couldn't get his order straight, and the service at the Mexican restaurant was slow. Life was constantly providing him with reasons to explode, and this made me so apprehensive. I understood that this temper of his was the evidence that he too was unhappy. He picks up on my 'you can't breathe to suit me' thoughts. He is not stupid. Like me, he doesn't know what to do with his life situation.

We had been back to our southwestern home on the Verde River only a few days when I finally got an appointment with a hypnotherapist Lyle recommended. What she told me had me feeling like I was in an altered state of consciousness as I drove myself up the canyon to Clarkdale. I didn't share anything with Brian over dinner, but I was careful to record everything she told me that night in my journal.

1. I attract men who love me very much. I do this because I NEED their love due to the fact that I didn't feel loved as a child.

2. I eventually start reacting to the husband's imperfections with criticism, mostly unspoken. I take on my mother's fault-finding ways because that is what was modeled for me.

3. I know that Daddy loved me, just like I know that every husband loves me. Yet, a man's love is not all that valuable to me because Daddy's love didn't protect me from Mother.

4. I don't really respect the 'being in love' condition because of my parents' example. My dad would take Mother's abuse in the name of loving her.

5. My unhappiness with Brian as my husband isn't about him. When I stop relating to him from my inner child (the subconscious part of my brain that noted Mother's behavior and accepted it as truth) and start interacting as 'Bonn, the adult', then I'll be able TO DETERMINE WHETHER HE SHOULD BE IN MY LIFE.

6. To do this I must change the way I think. Stop the 'what is wrong with him' thoughts, and substitute 'he is doing the best he can with what he knows'. In other words, see and honor the Christ within him (as with all people). When I am tempted to be critical, stop and tell myself that is Mother's way of thinking, and I am not her. I am Bonn, and I can come from a position of love with all people in my life.

As I closed my journal and turned off the light in my office, my thoughts preceded me into the bedroom. So now I have some new explanations of myself; some information I already knew about myself, and the question: Will today's time spent with the hypnotherapist make any difference in the way I live my life? Circles. My life of circles. Brian was watching TV, and I was glad that he had taken no interest in my silence since returning from Scottsdale.

A few days later I was taking a walk around Clarksdale when the garbage man stopped to tell me that there had been an attack on New York City. It was September 11. I ran all the way back to the house to tell Brian. His daughter Chris works in Manhattan, so we were very concerned. We sat glued to the TV all day, and after learning that it took Chris five hours to get home to New Jersey we finally gave up the day to the new reality we were now living. We sat on the patio in the dark, drinking a cocktail in silence. I didn't pose the question, but I was wondering if Brian too was thinking about how unfortunate it is that we can't be happy in our peaceful, beautiful home when today's evidence of the hatred in this world is so tragic. This being said, I realized that since my session in Scottsdale with the hypnotherapist I had a more detached way of looking at whatever comes up. Sometimes I actually felt like I was watching myself interact with Brian…sure was less emotional, if nothing else.

None of our friends or my son Lyle could go, but we went anyway. It was the middle of October and our two week research trip to Mexico to see if we would want to retire there proved to be turbulent. Lots of adventure: We unknowingly stayed in a motel whose main clientele was prostitutes and their customers for the evening. We finally figured it out when we couldn't find anything on TV except pornography; the food we ordered was delivered through a small opening in the wall, and each separate motel room had a garage door to hide the car. Then, there was the question of which road to take as we journeyed across the interior of Mexico. Few, if any signs left us depending on which way 'felt' right. The roads were horrible,and a blow out on one of our new tires held us up for hours out in the middle of nowhere. Physically it was no fun either. Brian got an eye infection and I got the infamous Mexican bug. Nevertheless, Brian loved the slow, uncomplicated life style of the American and Canadian people we met. I couldn't go because I was sick, but he went on without me to a dinner party in the retirement compound where we were staying for a few days. He came home so excited and full of all the wonderful details of living the life of an expat in Mexico. That and our noon meals of fish tacos and beer, followed by siesta time, and then sitting for hours in the plaza visiting with other senior citizens, had Brian ready to move there. Actually, it would be a perfect solution, was my thought, as we drove toward the Mexico Arizona border. Let Brian live out his idle days in Mexico, and I could stay in Arizona with my friends, Lyle, and my work. No divorce, just distance. Sounds good. I don't want family and friends to know I have once again failed at marriage. However, they probably all know that I have not married men I thought I loved and wanted in my life......that is, except for the father of my children. Instead, there has always been some need that I didn't think I could manage on my own, to push me down the aisle. Then, given a few years with my 'most recently selected vehicle of change', and I'm looking for a way out. Again, circles. Thanks to my current detached way of watching me live my life, I'm not crying about it or blaming Brian. What I do, I do.

I'm not sure of the exact moment when I decided to leave Brian, but as my nights became more sleep filled and my days less stressful I realized that it was because I had a plan. You remember, it's that 'beginnings' thing I like. Sort of like 'endings' too. Just don't put me in the middle for too long. I would move to Santa Fe where my sister LaVoyce was carving out her new life. Lyle would move me into a small apartment. I would get an education related position either with the public school district or the New Mexico Dept. of Education. That, with my Texas Teacher Retirement, I'd be good to go. I would give Brian half of my retirement money because he was responsible for helping me get it as quickly as I had. And, I was not suggesting divorce. I didn't need a divorce. I didn't want a divorce. I just wanted to have my life back so I could live it alone in Santa Fe.

Was he actually relieved when I told him? I almost think he was, especially when he so easily and quickly told me his plan. As was his habit, he was just waiting for the woman in his life to open the subject of divorce. His mother lived alone in Ohio, and she would be absolutely thrilled to have him join her. He could get a teaching job there and with his friends and brother close, it would be okay to be back into the world of his youth. That is, if he could get past the awful Ohio winter weather.

November the 28th, I was at home in my new digs. It had been a whirlwind of packing, selling furniture, moving to Santa Fe, but it was all done now. I found a tiny one bedroom adobe garage apartment on a large property that is typical Santa Fe. A psychologist from Germany lived in the large house with his wife who is an artist. Wow! New and interesting people to live around, but not with, and LaVoyce was only a few blocks away. My guides deserve an A+ for leading me in the right direction. I had not envisioned a nondescript apartment complex for this my next life, but a place with the imperfections that make for conversation. The kitchen was tiny, but its Mexican flavor made the little time I spent in it enjoyable. My rug covered the living room floor from wall to wall, thus making the room so cozy for my love seat and rocker in front of the TV. The bedroom was large enough for my desk, my queen bed and comfy chair, but oh my, the bathroom and closet were like nothing I had ever experienced before. I could stand in front of the sink to brush my teeth, then swing around to sit down on the commode, before taking one step into the shower. And, then there was the closet. It was deep, so all my clothes could hang. However, I could only move sideways along the wall of it to select my dress. The hangers were so close to my nose that it would almost make me nauseous if I took too much time deciding what to wear. These daily inconveniences made me really appreciate the motel rooms I got to stay in when I traveled for my new job. Early in the following year, as a New Mexico Department of Education consultant, my fellow workers and I had many laughs over how I looked forward to taking baths and being able to step back and see my clothes hanging in front of me in motel rooms.

Well, once again, I was living alone. I had just finished doing my transcendental meditation, and was now in my living room easy chair, drinking coffee and looking out the window at the lightly falling snow. Brian left for Ohio yesterday, and I was so glad to have him go. The fourteen days it took us to get moved out of Arizona wasn't a bad time, but the minute we hit Santa Fe, every reason I ever had for not wanting to be around him surfaced. His criticalness was in full bloom. He found fault with LaVoyce's choice for car insurance; he got mad at the telephone man who came to install my phone, and he watched a video taken of me in Houston when I was interviewed about *Higher Ground* and just got furious. He told me that my metaphysical approach to life was the reason for our problems. So much for ever thinking that during our years together he had understood anything I have ever had to say about the spiritual approach to life.

My reaction to Santa Fe was much like the one I had had to Sedona, AZ back in 1990. I felt reborn to a new environment of such majestic beauty; stimulating people were everywhere; fantastic Christmas gifts to purchase for all my Texas family I'll see soon, and no limit to available educational positions here in the capitol city. Having LaVoyce to hang out with too gave me the family feel everyone wants. Then, I discovered Sunday night dancing at the Paramount. Smoking was not allowed and ice water was free. Add to that, lots of friendly men and women to talk to and dance with. My favorite dance partner looked just like

Henry Fonda. I loved dancing with him because he didn't twirl me around. Some of the dancers made me dizzy, and I didn't like that. Give me a partner with a strong lead and good rhythm, and I'll end the evening happy and tired from the exercise that dancing is.

It also added to my happiness to know that Brian was doing well in Ohio. We talked on the phone at least once a week, and he reported that his life was settling into a pattern that worked for him. Hilda was beside herself with joy to have him under her roof. He bought the groceries and she cooked for him, and now she had a man on her arm for all the local social gatherings, church and lunch during the week at the Senior Center. He suspects that it makes her nervous to hear us laughing and talking on the phone because she doesn't ever want him to leave her. Too, his pursuit for a teaching job was in full swing, and he saw his brother John daily. I didn't miss him at all, and I was so happy to know that he was okay. I had a new line I used whenever the subject came up: "He is easier to love, than to live with." I got it from a movie LaVoyce and I went to see.

December always brings my birthday on the 4th and I am not known for doing my birthdays well. It isn't just the age thing either. I can remember sitting on the front porch steps in Nacogdoches when I was in college and just crying my eyes out. Therefore, my being 64 years old now can't be the whole story, but what it is, I've never figured out. This year I filled the day with solo activity: I spent the afternoon at the New Mexico Museum, then I did some more Christmas shopping. I had a sandwich and glass of wine at the Palace in downtown Santa Fe, and thoroughly enjoyed my solitude. Phone calls from all my children completed the day. My son Lyle and I made a plan to celebrate my birthday on the 10th when I would fly to Phoenix to go with him to hear Lee Carroll's lecture and be a witness to the Kryon channeling.

Carroll was speaking to a large audience, but it felt like he was talking to me directly when he said, "There is one here who has spent their life searching for love. Someone to fulfill their life. Their perfect mate, and it has not happened. That is because you don't realize that you are searching for the other part of yourself. You know you are eternal, that you can co-create with God, but you don't really believe it. Thus it doesn't get to your cellular level where real change occurs. Consequently, you don't become whole and complete within yourself. This causes you to attract the inappropriate people instead of the one who would compliment your life. As always, it is about you – not them."

I also noted what Carroll said about the people who died on Sept.11. He said that they are fine. Many of them are coming right back in as Indigos. Since the 1990's many children have been born as Indigos. I know my granddaughter Cody is Indigo. She has all the characteristics: traditional schooling is a challenge for her; she lives totally in the moment; she is hard to direct; she doesn't see consequences and she doesn't do guilt. I will talk to Jon, her dad, about this when I am in Texas for Christmas.

I took the occasion of sending out Christmas cards to include a letter to Brian's daughters, Chris and Cathy. The letters were identical.

"Dearest Cathy and Chris,

I have been composing this letter in my mind for days. There are very few family members (on both your dad and my sides) that I am offering an explanation to. Not having to justify or defend my decisions is one of the few perks of old age. Ha

It has been five years since Brian and I started our life together. Both of us brought to our relationship the desire, dream, demand that we be successful this time. That we not repeat our past (we both have three failed marriages). And I think that I can speak for both of us

127

when I say that we have given it an all out effort. However, as the years have rolled past, it has become obvious to us that we do not have the same agenda for our lives. That would not be a death blow to the marriage except that along with this fact....we are growing more intolerant of how the other 'shows up for life'. Instead of seeing that the other is only mirroring who we are, we have become critics of each other. Since neither of us are willing to give up who we are, that leaves us with a tension that robs our days of all happiness. We live in a beautiful world; travel to fun places, and enjoy good friends and loving families. Yet, because of our strained relationship, happiness together is a thing of the past.

Your dad's decision to move back to Ohio is a good one, I think. All the pluses are obvious: Hilda is thrilled to have him with her. John will now get some help with his mom, and it will make your dad feel good to shoulder some responsibility for her after all these many years. Maybe Brian can influence his brother John to go places with him and create a life for himself. He has close friends there that he enjoys. You and Chris are within a day's drive. He will now have the opportunity to share holidays and special occasions with you all. He will be handy to help you both with any home repair jobs. He can watch his grandchildren grow and be more to them than the grandfather who shows up once or twice a year. The only minus in this whole scenario is the bitter, long winters of Ohio. You know how your dad needs for his world to be inviting to outdoor life.

No one can predict how his life will go, but I fully support his decision to attempt this. With any luck, he will be fine. John told him this week of a teaching job possibility in a small town 20 miles from Hilda's. Margaret Ann, brother John's wife, is busy getting the way paved for him substituting there in Bristolville. They both seem very glad to have him coming there to live.

As for me, I will thrive in Santa Fe. I chose it for several reasons: My sister is here and we have always enjoyed each other. It is a small city without air pollution and I must have that for my lungs. It is a day's drive to my children Lyle, Summer and Jon. I love the atmosphere and energy here. It is large enough to offer cultural events, a good job market (being the state capitol, having two colleges and many private schools), and it is a beautiful place to live. I have rented a small garage apartment on a two acre estate only minutes from LaVoyce. It is the typical adobe hacienda, surrounded by coyote fencing. I have a carport for the car, a darling patio, and interesting neighbors. My plan is to start on my PhD in January. I am in full pursuit of a job in education, and since solitude has always been my friend, I should be okay.

I will continue to write you. I do so hope you will want to keep in touch with me. There is no predicting how things will go with your dad and I. As of now, we don't have any plan to divorce. Time will give us our best direction. Take care and I love you very much.

Bonn"

My all day trip to Texas for Christmas was wonderful. Being alone in a car driving through beautiful mountains and long stretches of nothing is one of my favorite things. And, the visit in the small town of Hallettsville where I spent twenty seven years of my life was predictable. My ex-husband's family is always gracious to me, but they do have a hard time with who I am. Since the publishing of *Higher Ground*, their suspicions around who and what I am are almost palpable. I didn't help matters either when I took it upon myself on Christmas Eve to give them the benefit of my views concerning the family split over inherited money. But, Jon and Cody riding back to Santa Fe with me to go skiing was the perfect finishing touch to my Texas holiday.

Cody slept on the couch, and Jon had a blow-up mattress on the floor beside her. For four days they went skiing, and I had the pleasure of their company for nightly dinners and TV. Cody won high praise from the ski instructor. She was tireless and so very strong. However, the one evening we decided to go out for Mexican food she was so tired that she almost napped while Jon braided her hair. It was a Friday night, and getting into a good Mexican restaurant was proving to be more of a problem than LaVoyce or I had anticipated. Finally, after going and then leaving three restaurants because the wait time was too long, Cody came out with one of her famous one-liners. We were getting out of the car when her Aunt LaVoyce told her that if we couldn't get into Castro's, we would go to Blakes Burgers close by on Rodeo Road. Cody's response was, "If we can't get in here, I'm going to say shit".

It took some effort on my part to get LaVoyce to agree to go out with me on New Years Eve. It was cold; she didn't want to get dressed up, and she didn't want to risk sitting all night without being asked to dance. Nevertheless, after some 'shame on you' from me, she relented. I have always celebrated New Years Eve by getting all dressed up and going out dancing. Jon and Cody would be staying in because Cody was excited about making what she called a romantic dinner for her dad. She had lit and placed every candle in my apartment on the small table with a pizza. I was all fluffed and ready to go by the time LaVoyce arrived. She had on the same thing she had worn to Mike's wedding and she looked ravishing. There was no doubt as to who would be left sitting at the table alone at the La Fonda Hotel, where we were going to hear the band.

It was one of those magical nights. My sister and I had often gone dancing throughout the years, and it doesn't always happen this way. But tonight, all was perfect. We hadn't been there long when two men asked us to join them at their table. It was a very crowded place, and everyone was in a holiday mood. The music was good; our wine was purchased by the gentlemen; one of them was a good dancer, and LaVoyce was the belle of the ball. We both had a very good time, and as we drove back to my apartment, we congratulated ourselves on our good fortune.

"I bet he calls you."

Surprisingly, LaVoyce wasn't all that interested. "Maybe so." was all she said. Neither of us, at the time when January 1st was only an hour old, could have guessed that a memorable romance would develop for her in 2002 with tonight's dance partner.

As I walked into my warm apartment where my son and granddaughter were sleeping, I was filled with the joy of being alive. I had had a very good time dancing and visiting with strangers. I was thrilled that it was my sister and not me who now had a possible love interest. A new man was last on my list of needs. As I shed my dancing dress and got washed up for bed, my lifelong temptation to spend my time trying to figure out every problem – be it personal, social, financial – the seduction behind my belief that I can engineer a solution, was not happening tonight. No, I told myself, as I climbed into my comfortable bed, my only New Year's resolution is to not let fear have a great authority over my life during this new year. And, I thought sleepily, as I closed my eyes and listened to the wind howling outside my window, if there is an answer to why I live circles, I'm not all that interested. Not tonight, anyway.

Brian Berwald
Daughters: Chris and Cathy
Grandchildren: Lindsay, Jenna, Nina, and Dylan

Photograph by Robin Levin